GW00750948

GRANDPARENTS CRY TWICE:
Help for Bereaved Grandparents

Mary Lou Reed

Baywood Publishing Company, Inc.
AMITYVILLE, NEW YORK

Library of Congress Catalog Number: 99-34925
ISBN: 0-89503-204-X

Library of Congress Cataloging-in-Publication Data

Reed, Mary Lou, 1934-
    Grandparents cry twice : help for bereaved grandparents / Mary Lou Reed.
        p.   cm.
    Includes bibliographical references and index.
    ISBN 0-89503-204-X (alk. paper)
        1. Bereavement- -Psychological aspects. 2. Grandchildren- -Death-
    -Psychological aspects. 3. Grandparents- -Psychology. 4. Reed, Mary
    Lou, 1934-   . I. Title.
    BF575.G7R44   1999
    155.9' 37' 0853- -dc21   99-34925
                                                                        CIP

In Loving Memory of Alexander
December 30, 1986 – June 17, 1989

Grief waves strike my heart
Time eases, not erases
Glory clouds trailing
Brought joy, then pain

A life too short
Forever, we remember
A boy of two
Beloved, Alexander.

Grandma Reed

Prologue

LETTERS FOR CURTIS

It was there when we returned from the funeral—a manila envelope covered with bright stickers, propped next to the front door. The package contained condolence letters addressed to my grandson Curtis. They had been written by his third-grade classmates.

The past several months had been a time of mixed and often confusing experiences for our family—especially for Curtis. He enjoyed playing with his little brother Alex but was thrilled when his baby sister Stephanie arrived that spring. New siblings create a need for adjustments. Before Curtis and his family could settle into a new routine, however, Alex fell ill and was hospitalized. So critically ill was Alex that we celebrated Curtis' ninth birthday in a small room at the hospital. Alex's illness, hospitalization, and subsequent death a week after the birthday party produced emotions that were overwhelming, not only for Curtis, but for all of us.

The death of my precious grandson devastated me, and our entire family, although our individual reactions and feelings were all different. The special relationship each of us had with Alex colored our responses as much as did our separate personalities. His death, out of the natural order of life, brought grief, confusion, and anger. Alex's untimely death also made it difficult for relatives and friends to express their love, care, and concern.

Some comments, made with the best of intentions, actually added to our grief and turmoil. Perhaps the cruelest remarks

v

made to our family were those suggesting there would be other children in the future. How were they to know that statement would be true? More importantly, another child can never replace the one who died.

During our initial anguish, we were to discover how expressions of consolation on the death of a child could be not only troublesome, but treacherous. Armored adult feelings seemed to hamper the expression of sincere solace, resulting in stiff and formal condolences. It was then, with some degree of hesitation and trepidation, that we opened the envelope left for Curtis at the front door.

> Dear Curtis, I am so sorry that your brother died. I hope you can come to school soon the class misses you alot. I am so sorry that when I heard about it I was crying. Curtis it is all right to cry. . . . We miss you here at school. We want you to come back. Tell your family that it is ok to cry. Curtis it is ok.

Simple, direct, heartfelt. With the spontaneity of youth, this child encouraged crying. We found most "don't" statements, such as "Don't cry," to be inappropriate. In our suffering, we believed in doing what we needed to do to survive. Our family considers crying to be an appropriate and healing response to loss, as are anger, sadness, fear, and frustration. This young letter-writer gave us permission to experience and express our natural feelings. Many of the letters included drawings and pictures, as did this one, of a sad face with tears streaming down, and a cartoon caption: "It's ok to cry," this letter spoke eloquently to our family's needs and sorrow.

The letters were written the week following Alex's death, a class assignment the last week of school that spring, a week Curtis did not attend. Many of the children wrote about their plans for summer and how they would be available to play with Curtis. Few of the letters had correct composition, spelling, and punctuation; but that did not detract from the strength of their message. It was the absence of guile and the naive approach to the art of condolence that we found so endearing.

> . . . I know what your asking to yourself why my brother. there are people out in the open that are going to make fun of you but I won't. when my grandpa died I cried cry all you want.

This youngster stated the agonizing why question we all felt in all our hearts. A separate cover for this letter depicted a sun, dark cloud, and down the left hand side, in bold, dark letters, "Sorrowful, Annoyed, Darn sad."

The pictures were frequently as touching and insightful as the words themselves. The symbolism of the drawings would probably require a professional to fully interpret. We, the grieving family, simply appreciated and accepted them on an emotional level. Many of the pictures included sun and clouds. Several pictures included drawings of wave-like ground. The meaning of the wavy ground became obvious in one letter as the artist had printed around the outside of the design: "Even thow things are in a slump the'll straiten out some how."

In his accompanying letter he wrote of sorrow and hope, but with words reminiscent of adult comments.

> I am sorry about your brother. It's going to be hard to get over but you'll get over it some how. I'll be there to help you if you want. I know your coverd with clouds but some how the sun will come threw.

Several of the letter-writers used words, and indicated attitudes about death, they probably learned from their families. One such letter included a picture of the sun, clouds, a rainbow, and flowers. It contained a personal experience of a death in the family and ended with a slight word twist on an old philosophy of life.

> I'm so sorry that your brother pasted away. When I first heard the news I felt very sad. I feel very sorry for you. when I was five in august my grandma pasted away from

cansar, I felt very sad but then after about a month or so I tired to get over it. It helped. But everything in life lives and goes.

Those who write about recent death experiences in their families often did so with what we felt was a fascinating directness of feeling. Many, however, also made statements mimicking adult condolences.

> I hope you feel better soon and come back to class you do have friends and all you need to do if you want to play with someone is ask I also hope this letter makes you feel a lot better. I'm sorry this had to happen I know how you feel I felt like that when my Gramps and Grama died of Canser.

"I know how you are feeling," we heard frequently from adults. We felt that comment ignored the very private experience of our emotions. Whatever one's reaction and response to a death, no matter how similar the circumstance, I believe it to be individual and different for each person.

The general, and what must be considered genuine, concern expressed by the children for Curtis "feeling better" was frequently mixed with the message of "be happy."

> Dear Curtis, I am very sorry that your brother died, I know you feel bad but it will pass over when my aunt died I was very sad to but I got strong and now I think of her but I smile. So Don't worry, Be Happy!

The picture on this letter with its sun, black clouds, rain, rainbow, and flowers sprouting from the earth is a lovely reflection of the author's written message. A number of the children wrote about their concern for Curtis "feeling better" or "being happy," but only one attempted poetry.

> Dear Curtis, I wanted to write a little poem to make you feel happy sowe here it is. roses are red violets are blue I now you miss your brother sowe do I to.

Using both written and pictorial processes, the children spoke the unspoken in a manner most adults would envy. Their open declaration of thoughts and feelings offered wonderful and sorely needed comfort to us.

> Curtis I am sorry about your brother. I wish you still had him. He must have been a great brother. Your my friend. I think that you should have a brother. I am sad. about what happened. Your a great person. I wouldn't want my brother to die if I were you . . .

All of the letters were appreciated then, and continue to be cherished. The letters gave Curtis not only something he could read, but vital support from his peers. The thoughtfulness of the teacher's assignment and the timing of the arrival of the packet of letters were of immeasurable comfort to all of us. What, after all, does one do following a funeral? The mourning had barely begun. Bereft of our precious Alex, Curtis and the rest of us staggered under the load of our enormous grief. All of the adult condolences and the funeral ritual could not, did not, address our grief as well as the young girl who simply and directly spoke to the family's sorrow and incomprehension on the death of their beloved two-year-old.

> I fell very sad your little brother dieing. I hope you fell beter. You are a very good friend and I really fell bad for you. Your little brother is very nice and so little to die. **I think he died too early.**

TABLE OF CONTENTS

Introduction 1

Chapter 1
My Grandson's Life and Death 5

Chapter 2
Our Family's Grief 11

Chapter 3
My Search for Help 21

Chapter 4
The Grief Process 29

Chapter 5
Helping Myself 43

Chapter 6
Helping Our Grieving Child 55

Chapter 7
Sibling Grief and Needs 63

Chapter 8
In Memory: Memorials and Healing Rituals . . . 73

Chapter 9
How Others May Help/Hinder 83

Chapter 10
Finding My Way 93

Epilogue 103

Appendix I: Selected Poems 105

Appendix II: Resources 117

Bibliography 121

Index 125

INTRODUCTION

By loving I risked loss. When I lost Alex, my beloved grandson, I experienced crushing grief. If you are reading this book following the death of a loved one, please know that my love and heart go out to you. Whatever your circumstances, I hope this book will help you understand that you are not alone.

This book is written from my viewpoint as a sorrowing grandparent with the intention that by sharing the particulars of my grief and sadness I might touch the universal in all our bereavement. Thus, in some small way perhaps you, the reader, may find a correlation to your own situation, and thus gain comfort and strength.

Writing this book has been an act of love and remembering, a way of finding some peace for my broken heart following Alex's death. Compounding my grief was the realization that I had lost my son, David, as he had been, for he would never be the same. My world had suddenly become not only painful, but dark, confusing, and scary.

My enormous sense of loss seemed different from others I had experienced. What made Alex's death so agonizing? Was the grief of a grandparent for a grandchild different somehow? Or did it come from the dual loss I was experiencing?

Neither family, friends, nor faith had answers for me. More often than not, their only messages were words like, "It's God's plan," Those words seemed not only incomprehensible, but often infuriating.

1

I turned to books, where historically I had found answers and refuge. Not much could be found about grandparents in grief literature. Fortunately, I eventually found that from poetry, ancient myths, personal anecdotes, and even in contemporary fiction I could find words of wisdom and solace, and a kind of companionship through my grief.

In the beginning, however, I needed a more concrete method of pain-reduction, a way of sorting out my confused feelings. I started writing, doing what Shakespeare suggested, "Give sorrow words; the grief that does not speak whispers the o'er fraught heart and bids it break." My first journal—in an old, partially used spiral notebook—soon filled up and I bought more notebooks and continued to write.

Eventually my journal writing coalesced into more organized writing which led to this book. It has not been easy. Writing and crying at the same time, while healing, I found exhausting. And then there were the decisions of what to share and what not to share. Some of my grief experiences must remain private—pieces that will protect my son and his family's privacy, and memories that I wish to hold private. Also, I chose not to make an attempt at discussing the particular concerns of grandfathers and the religious issues involved with death and grieving.

Many people known and unknown to me have assisted in this work. A few people's contributions, however, are rather tenuous. I prefer to think of those as "passing in the night" encounters. Although those experiences for the most part felt extremely negative, I have come to learn how they helped define who I now am.

From my personal experiences and from my extensive research, I have come to believe that there are people and organizations who can assist us, personal resources we can call on, authorities we can consult, and perhaps most importantly personal choices we can make to help us find our way through our grief.

Listed in the bibliography are those resources supplied by numerous authors and academic materials not cited in the text. Some of the longest and most supportive assistance came from the kind and long-suffering friends in my writer's group. Over the years many have come and gone, but all have left their mark. I appreciate all of them. My special thanks go to Dr. G. Lynn Nelson, Professor of English at Arizona State University, and author of *Writing and Being* [1, p. 13]. His statement that writing is a "tool—an emotional, intellectual, and spiritual tool—to help you survive and grow and find meaning and purpose and peace in your life," has become an anchor for me since Alex died.

His death became a defining point of my life. But my story is different from yours. We are all complex beings, we bring our diverse personalities, values, and experiences to our grieving. Our feelings will be unique despite their universal connections. Writing this book helped me touch those connections—that shared ground of knowing that I will never be who I once was, nor the person I am yet to become, for mourning is a journey, a constant reminder that things are now different.

REFERENCE

1. G. L. Nelson, *Writing and Being,* Lura Media, San Diego, California, 1994.

Chapter 1

MY GRANDSON'S LIFE AND DEATH

The Soul that rises with us, our life's Star,
Hath had elsewhere its setting,
And cometh from afar:
Not in entire forgetfulness,
And not in utter nakedness,
But trailing clouds of glory . . . [1, p. 348].

William Wordsworth

On a shelf above my computer I keep a photograph of my grandson Alexander holding his newborn sister, Stephanie, both enclosed in their mother Andrea's arms. Alex looks directly out of that photo and seems to make eye contact with me. Most days I enjoy looking at that picture. Often my heart hurts. It is the last photograph I took of Alex before he died on Saturday, June 17, 1989. The next day was Father's Day.

Born December 30, 1986, the second son of my second son, David, Alex appeared at birth, and for more than two years, to be a healthy baby with no evidence of his fatal genetic defect. His strawberry blonde hair and large blue eyes made him a poster boy in this grandma's eyes. At birth, and throughout his too short life, I thought Alex to be perfect, the consummate example of Wordsworth's suggestion that we come, "trailing clouds of glory." If anyone doubts that statement, he has only to verify it with all the people I badgered with photos and anecdotes.

5

I had eagerly awaited Alex's birth as he was to be the first new baby for our family in almost seven years. Starr, the daughter of my eldest son, had just turned eight. Curtis, David and Andrea's first child, was six-and-a-half years old. I already felt blessed with two grandchildren as the Christmas holiday season approached in 1986. Since David and Andrea expected their new baby close to the first of the year, my husband, Frank, and I decided to travel to California to celebrate the holidays with them. Frank needed to return to work shortly after Christmas, but Alex's maternal grandfather, Jim, and I remained to await the new baby's birth.

Alex and his mother came home the first day of January 1987—an exciting way to celebrate the beginning of the New Year. We all enjoyed holding, talking, and singing to Alex, and sometimes just leaning over the crib to watch him sleep. Holding him and rocking in front of the fireplace while listening to Mozart remains one of my fondest memories of those first days of his life.

Curtis' excited anticipation and then his enjoyment of his sibling became a source of mutual satisfaction for both boys and many photo opportunities for me. As Alex grew and developed, our enjoyment with him did not fade. He was a bright, amusing, and charming child. Our sense of delight in him came, not only due to our long wait for his arrival, but because of his sweet and beguiling personality. He also slept all night most nights, and as his father would say, "he wakes up happy." On one of my visits I awoke to babbling baby sounds as Alex played in his crib (he would play with his crib toys for a long time in the mornings). I took him out of his crib to snuggle with me in my bed. Curtis joined us there, and the three of us made a lasting memory.

During Alex's first year, his parents lived in an area close to a rugged canyon park. Curtis and I derived immense joy from the enchanting times with Alex out in his stroller, bouncing over the rough, leaf-strewn ground. Alex's obvious thrill with the trips and his interest in the natural world made those trips special. Even as a small baby Alex seemed to see incredibly well and responded with excitement to all sorts of sights, especially birds and planes in the sky.

Alex loved the outdoors, also a favorite place of mine. The hummingbird exhibit at the San Diego Zoo enchanted both of us. He also visited our home when his family traveled to our home during the Christmas holidays of 1988. That trip gave me great pleasure and ultimately became the only time Alex visited our house. My memory of Alex being in our home remains important to me.

During his short life, Alex had the opportunity to experience a number of unusual places and events. For a child growing up in southern California, Alex had the rare adventure of seeing a snowstorm. The storm occurred during the period I stayed with him and Curtis (in February prior to his death in June) while their parents attended a business meeting. The boys and I often went to a local park to play when Curtis came home from school. One of those days we chased snowflakes. Alex ran about and squealed with happiness while trying to catch the elusive flakes, looking in surprise at the wet spot left when he did. The next morning we awoke to a winter wonderland of snow. Covering trees, bushes, and ground, the snow brought an expression of amazement and questioning to Alex's big blue eyes.

One of my most poignant recollections of Alex comes from when he was about six months old. While I held him, his mother and I, both RNs, talked about some of our maternity ward experiences. I clearly remember commenting, "With all the things that can go wrong it is amazing how often babies are born perfect, like this one." We had no suspicion of what would eventually happen to our perfect baby.

When baby Stephanie arrived on April 29, 1989, the family rejoiced. Alex would say, "My baby" as he hovered over her. Soon after I had returned home from being with his family for Stephanie's birth, Alex became ill with cold/flu-like symptoms. One evening his parents called to tell us he had spiked a very high fever. We were all alarmed. I can still remember the stab of cold fear I felt in my heart.

Diagnosed originally as having an ear infection and placed on antibiotics, Alex improved somewhat—a pattern that would continue until the last day of his life. In this day of modern medicine and antibiotics, we were confident he would get well. The physician treating Alex assured his parents, "It's just a virus." When the high fever returned and he became sicker, he was diagnosed as having mononucleosis caused by the Epstein-Barr virus. Supportive-care only was prescribed, because, the doctor said, "a viral infection has to run its course." Alex improved somewhat, then again got sicker. When examined on May 31, he was dehydrated; the doctor felt he needed to be hospitalized. Following Alex's admittance to a local hospital, a routine blood examination revealed he had *no* white blood cells. He was transferred immediately to a hospital with a critical care unit.

Numerous tests were done the day following Alex's admittance to Pediatric Intensive Care. Large amounts of antibiotics and whole blood were administered, since he had, for all intents, no immune system at that moment and had two streptococcus infections superimposed on the mononucleosis. Leukemia was considered. A bone marrow biopsy proved negative. That good news, received three days after Alex's admittance and on his parents' wedding anniversary, seemed propitious; and our hopes rose.

Because some people develop a severe hepatitis as Alex did from mononucleosis, there is a small mortality rate, but Alex seemed well on his way to recovering after only four days in Intensive Care. He was moved to a ward bed, but his fever and diarrhea continued unabated, which was certainly enough to make anyone exhausted and irritable as he continued to be. When he did not improve after a week and then had some respiratory difficulties stemming from his enlarged liver and fluid in his abdomen, he was readmitted to Pediatric Intensive Care. Further tests were done, experts were consulted. We were all frightened.

At this time a suspicion of a genetic defect began to be discussed. Andrea had had a brother die about thirty years earlier at about the same age as Alex from an undiagnosed infection, despite antibiotics. Unable to reverse the effects of the Epstein-Barr infection, or to make a definitive diagnosis, Alex's doctors considered the possibility Alex suffered from x-linked lymphoproliferative disease. Also known as Duncan's syndrome, it is a disease with a 100 percent fatality rate for infants. (It would be a year after Alex died before a definitive diagnosis was made.) The genetic defect had made it impossible for Alex to develop any antibodies to the Epstein-Barr virus that overran his body.

During Alex's hospitalization, we saw many children admitted and discharged from Pediatric Intensive Care. We were witnesses to the incredible, searing grief of parents whose child had died from drowning. We often became bystanders to the drama and the frenetic pace of a full Pediatric Intensive Care, and the seemingly near-miraculous recoveries of seriously-ill children. We had expected no less for Alex. It was not to be.

A little over two weeks after his admittance to the hospital, Alex had a seizure on Thursday morning and became unconscious. As his systems degenerated, the medical personnel worked valiantly to save his life. Unfortunate side effects of those efforts included swelling of his head, and the extreme imbalance in his blood chemistry caused bleeding. When I went to visit him on Friday evening, I found David reading a book to Alex and wiping blood from his nostrils. It is an image that will remain forever in my memory.

By Saturday evening, Alex's body could no longer sustain his spirit. When all the heroics proved futile, the medical staff undid all the tubes and lines and lifted Alex into David's arms to hold. Just as they did that, his weary little heart stopped. David sat and held him for quite some time and we each had an opportunity to touch, stroke, smell him, and tell him how much we loved him.

Alex had given us something very precious; contact with the love within us. When he died, however, I felt like I had been dropped into a pit of unspeakable emotions. How could Alex's parents, brother Curtis, and baby Stephanie endure this terrible loss? How were we going to survive?

REFERENCE

1. W. Wordsworth, Ode: Intimations of Immortality from Recollections of Early Childhood, in *A Treasury of the Familiar,* Consolidated Book Publishers, Chicago, 1942.

Chapter 2

OUR FAMILY'S GRIEF

... And as he was dreaming, an angel song
    Awakened our Little Boy Blue
Oh, the years are many, the years are long,
    But the little toy friends are true.

Aye, faithful to Little Boy Blue they stand,
    Each in the same old place,
Awaiting the touch of a little hand,
    And the smile of a little face.
And they wonder, as waiting these long years through,
    In the dust of that little chair,
What has become of our Little Boy Blue
    Since he kissed them and put them there [1, p. 603].

Eugene Field

How we longed to feel "the touch of a little hand" and see "the smile of a little face." Stunned by the enormity of our loss, we not only "wondered" but wandered.

With great difficulty, we packed Alex's clothes, blankets and toys, our belongings, and numerous other things accumulated during those two-and-a-half weeks David, Andrea, baby Stephanie and I lived in a hospital room to be near Alex. I drove one of their cars on that long trip to their home. Curtis rode with me, and I was glad to have him.

I have always felt emotionally close to my son's family. When Curtis was born they had lived in the same city as us and Andrea's parents. Several years after Curtis' birth, Andrea's mother died, and I became "mom" to both Andrea and David. When they moved to another state, I helped them move and then visited there often.

During my life I had been proud of my supporting capabilities as a wife, mother, grandmother, and nurse. Now, following Alex's death, my own hurt felt terrifying. The helplessness I felt watching my son and daughter-in-law's anguish compounded my sense of inadequacy. My powerlessness to even mollify, much less alleviate, the pain from their incomprehensible loss heightened my sense of confusion. A long way from home, I felt isolated, bewildered, and overwhelmed.

Unable to soften my children's suffering, all I could think to do was continue to be with them and attend to the necessary routines of life. With Andrea's father with us, we had four adults and two children in the house, and my husband was on the way. Ordinary tasks such as unpacking, laundry, and food-preparation seemed essential.

"There is a reason women cook in the presence of death," mystery writer Christine Andreae says, "why we bake hams and zucchini bread and cupcakes brightly dotted with M&Ms for the children. It not only grounds us in the deepest rhythms of life, it is also a discipline and, like any discipline, it can serve as a shield" [2, p. 45]. While I did not "bake hams and zucchini bread and cupcakes," I kept busy doing routine chores. Laundry, cleaning up the house, answering phone calls, and taking care of Curtis and baby Stephanie helped to shield me from the horror of Alex's death.

His death could not be denied constantly, however. One example of coming face-to-face with the reality of his death often involved caring for baby Stephanie. Andrea and I had sorted Alex's baby clothes in preparation for her arrival. Often when we went to dress her, we wound find those clothes, and weep. Amidst our agony, however, baby Stephanie continued to be a constant source of love.

My emotions fluctuated those first hours and days after Alex's death, between the joy and wonder of our newborn Stephanie and what felt like annihilating pain. When I wasn't actively grieving for Alex, I ached for my children. Later I found a poem expressing those emotions:

The stars are not wanted now; put out every one,
Pack up the moon and dismantle the sun,
Put away the ocean and sweep up the woods;
For nothing now can ever come to any good [3, p. 141].

When I found David sobbing on Alex's bed, the break in my heart opened wider. And then it broke some more when I watched David carry Alex's tricycle up to his room. He had just learned to ride it while we awaited Stephanie's arrival.

David's action proved useful. Everywhere we found innumerable reminders of Alex—a toy, a book, a shoe, a coat, a cup, photos. We followed David's example by picking up those articles and putting them in Alex's room. We soon became aware of John Irving's meaning:

When someone you love dies, and you're not expecting it, you don't lose (him) all at once; you lose (him) in pieces over a long time—the way the mail stops coming, and (his) scent fades from the pillows and even from the clothes in (his) closet and drawers. Gradually, you accumulate the parts of (him) that are gone. Just when the day comes—when there's a particular missing part that overwhelms you with the feeling that (he's) gone, forever—there comes another day, and another specifically missing part [4, p. 135].

Our loss had many missing parts. The house held echoes of Alex. We would think we heard him; he had often tried to sneak out of the house, so we had monitored the doors diligently. His laughter, energy, smiles, and, more importantly, his love were what we missed immediately.

Soon we discovered the torment of "little firsts," as I call them, the first time going to the local store, community pool, favorite park, and what seemed like a million other places, without him. The day after Alex's funeral we all sort of wandered around and finally someone suggested we go to the community pool. We didn't last long there in that semi-public area with happy, laughing children around. David said he simply couldn't sit there as he missed chasing Alex around the pool.

The pain and agony of true anniversaries—birthday, death date, and all kinds of holidays, would come later. For a long time, however, I was acutely aware of weekly anniversaries. Alex had died on a Saturday evening. For our culture Saturday nights often have special meaning and now, for me, it held a cruel significance.

Often I felt that the center of my being had disappeared— a disorienting and painful perception. Ideas, beliefs, and assumptions about the world I had trusted, and had faith in, were no longer adequate. How could this have happened?

At some level, I am certain I anticipated Alex's condition would improve once Grandma was with him. That notion in no way suggests his parents did not love him with all their heart, nor that they did not do everything possible to protect him from harm. My belief was part of my trust in my personal and professional competence and simply a Grandma thing.

I will be eternally grateful for the privilege of being near and often with Alex during his last days. Due to both Andrea and I being RNs, and also our persistence in asking questions, we were able to obtain information that is not always available to lay people in those types of circumstances. As I watched Alex's valiant struggle to live, I understood on a rational level the biological circumstances. That did not alter my questioning his death. I wanted his spirit to live.

Not until after his death, however, did I realize how many hopes and dreams I had assigned to Alex. Now, not only were those hopes and dreams irretrievably shattered, but what had been my basic conjecture of how the world works was replaced with confusion.

As we struggled to understand Alex's death, exhausted and devastated, we moved, at times minute by minute, through the days between Alex's death and his funeral. Although my son and daughter-in-law were new to the area, Alex had been baptized in the church where his funeral was held. A death ceremony for a small child is always difficult. Alex's funeral was notably so for me. Raised in the Protestant faith, I have nevertheless attended many a Catholic funeral performed with dignity, offering consolation and hope. Alex's funeral gave me neither.

While Alex's parents sat close to the tiny white coffin and wept, the priest pontificated at great length, and at great physical distance from them. His remarks were, at best, doctrinaire. One of his comments angered me. He spoke of the biblical analogy of the sparrow falling to the ground, and said, *"although never having accomplished anything in this life,"* the sparrow was nevertheless important to the Holy Father. Alex accomplished many things during his short life, the most significant being the love he brought to all of us.

In all charity, our family decided that being old and obviously of a foreign descent, the priest may have been confused and even thought that the funeral was for a stillbirth. His confusion probably should not have been a surprise. No one from the church had called the hospital or David and Andrea's home, despite David's call to the church to advise them of Alex's critical condition during our long Saturday vigil. David was told that the priest could not visit the hospital that afternoon or evening because he had two weddings that day.

No one from the church ever phoned or visited my son's family, offering help in any manner—activities I have long associated with my religious affiliation. Someone experiencing a death in ancient, and even pre-industrial cultures, was nourished in the context of clan, tribe, or extended family. Such functions in our society are usually filled by members of religious institutions. Fortunately, an RN friend of my daughter-in-law's took on the responsibility of organizing friends and neighbors. They assisted our family with the thoughtful and greatly-appreciated support consistent with what I consider traditional care. Visits brought assurances of being available for whatever we might need, and a hot meal every day for a week. Since Andrea was still nursing Stephanie, it was vitally important for her, as well as for all of us, to have that kind of concern and support.

Not everyone was so supportive. Our world had stopped. Raw emotions gave us very little leeway to tolerate the thoughtlessness of a careless remark, attitudes, or behavior. Old wounds were easily rubbed raw. One of mine had been the failure of Alex's grandfather (my former husband) to put forth the time and energy to ever meet Alex. He did come to the funeral, but his lack of thoughtfulness at the luncheon following the funeral added to my misery and reawakened old irritations.

My husband, Frank, and I were a little late getting to the luncheon as we had taken flowers back to the house and checked on baby Stephanie, who was being cared for by a neighbor. When we arrived at the luncheon, we found David, Andrea, Curtis, Andrea's father and brother, and my former husband, next to my son, with his wife, seated at one table. There appeared to have been no thought or provision made for a place, even at another table, for us. Exhausted, despairing, and feeling overloaded with hurt, my cavalier remark to my son regarding the situation only added more stress and pain.

Although I had attended many funerals and the meals following such rituals, I had no recollection of anyone discussing post-funeral activities. Our return to David and Andrea's house seemed like walking into a vacuum. The presence of the third-grade students' letters (see Prologue) gave us desperately needed comfort with their simple, direct words of compassion. Later, in an attempt to fill time and distract ourselves, we finally spent several hours playing Trivial Pursuit.

When Frank and I prepared to leave, two days after the funeral, David and Andrea expressed fear about what was going to happen to them. They wanted us to stay longer. The enormity of my children's loss was incredible, and I felt great concern for their welfare. Over three weeks had transpired, however, since I had made the quick trip to Alex's bedside. I knew that I would not be of much help to anyone if I did not take care of myself. I needed to go home.

Exhausted, confused, and disoriented, I nevertheless attempted to return to some semblance of my regular routine. Normal chores such as grocery shopping, however, proved treacherous at times. Turning a corner in a store and suddenly seeing a boy Alex's age would instantly renew my stabbing pain and render me useless for the rest of the day. It did not take long to become aware of how different my world felt. My usual way of relating to those around me no longer felt comfortable or true. Social chit chat became an enormous irritant to me, and I felt no one wanted to listen to my tale of sorrow. Attempting to respond authentically to my feelings seemed to isolate me. I sensed many people were waiting for me to return to my usual self.

I knew intuitively I would never be the same. What and who I had been no longer existed. What had been routine thoughts escaped me. What I saw, heard, and felt seemed only vaguely recognizable in this new, changed world. There had been a dissolution of meaning, a shattering of my cherished assumptions. At times I felt I was floating in a void. My familiar anchors to the world had changed and were no longer recognizable, touchable, or even visible. I wandered. My landscape of being had changed, and I came to appreciate a statement by a character in Larry McMurtry's book, *Some Can Whistle*:

> The rules of happiness are as strict as the rules of sorrow; indeed, perhaps more strict. The two states have different densities, I've come to think. The lives of happy people are dense with their own doings—crowded, active, thick—urban, I would almost say.
>
> But the sorrowing are nomads, on a plain with few landmarks and no boundaries; sorrow's horizons are vague and its demands few. Jeannie and I had not become strangers; it was just that she lived in the city and I lived on the plain [5, p. 368].

I was a nomad. Where was I to turn? Where might I find some direction, a place to tie myself, to heal from the devastating wound of Alex's death? My emotions felt nearly impossible to express. The "what ifs" and the "whys" of his death threaded in and through my pain and anger. My usual interests seemed totally irrelevant, and often I simply needed distraction from my grief. My feelings vacillated between wanting to be alone and wanting someone with me. While I had any number of people say, "I'll call and we'll go to lunch," few ever did, and my ennui made it all but impossible to initiate that type of activity.

David and I had always had sports as a common interest. As big basketball fans he and I had kept a tenuous contact with the outside world through watching some of the NBA finals during the time Alex was hospitalized. In such a way we distracted ourselves for short periods of time from what was happening to Alex. A much more dramatic reminder of the fact that the world was going about its business were the news broadcasts of the activities occurring in Tiannamen Square.

At home, alone after Alex's death, day-time TV broadcasts of baseball games became my daily companion in my grief. It does not require a great deal of either mental or emotional energy to watch baseball. It was the perfect antidote for me.

When I did make an effort to talk to someone about my sorrow, I found it difficult. My other children wanted attention from me for their normal activities and problems. They were immersed in their own lives, but my mentioning of Alex's death would frighten them with the realization of their children's vulnerability.

Often when attempting to communicate with family, friends, and acquaintances, I found many would deny me my grief. There were the well-meaning people who said, "But you have other grandchildren, don't you?" "You will grow from this," "He is better off in heaven," "Enjoy what you have," "Just forget about it," and "I thought you would be over that by now." Those individuals failed, I believe, to either honor or realize the breadth and depth of my injury, the wound that was producing my angry, disconcerting feelings. As Judith Viorst wrote: "We are angry at the doctors for not saving them. We are angry at God for taking them away. Like Job, or the man in the following poem, we are angry at our comforters—what right have they to say that time will heal, God is good, it is all for the best, you'll get over it?"

Your logic, my friend, is perfect,
Your moral most drearily true;
But, since the earth closed on (his) coffin,
I keep hearing that—and not you [6, pp. 268-269].

"Time will heal" remarks particularly sounded like empty counsel. Almost anyone can bear even excruciating pain, if they know it will last only a certain span of time. To conceive of myself, or my children, being able to tolerate our suffering for a lengthy time seemed impossible. We were not comforted by the advice that our mourning would take many years, and perhaps a lifetime. We were incapable to see beyond our immediate distress in the early, intense phase of our grief.

My fierce, angry emotions of initial grief sometimes frightened me. Physical activity became, as it so often had in the past, a healing act. Tennis became an immense help. Striking the ball gave me a way to express my frustration and anger. Pounding walls and kicking things worked also, and the following poem still offers succor.

Just what he had against it I can't say
It was a harmless-looking box enough
That he was treating in a shameful way,
Kicking it ahead of him with rough
Enthusiastic kicks, with such a fierce
Impetuous joy, it seemed as if his toe
Was surely bound, with each kick, to pierce
Right through the cardboard side. It didn't though,
And he kept kicking at it out of sight
And getting happier with every kick
Like all of us who watched him with delight.
We'd been hurt too. We'd been hurt to the quick,
And we were eased of angers and of shocks
By every kick he gave that empty box [7].

Kicking an empty box felt like a sensible and relatively benign technique for relieving my pain and anger.

REFERENCES

1. E. Field, Little Boy Blue, *A Treasury of the Familiar,* Consolidated Book Publishers, Chicago, 1944.
2. C. Andreae, *Grizzly,* St. Martin's Press, New York, 1994.
3. E. Mendelson (ed.), Funeral Blues, in *W. H. Auden, Collected Poems,* Random House, New York, 1940.
4. J. Irving, *A Prayer for Owen Meany,* Ballantine Books, New York, 1989.
5. L. McMurtry, *Some Can Whistle,* Simon & Schuster, New York, 1989.
6. J. Viorst, *Necessary Losses,* Ballantine Books, New York, 1987.
7. J. Merchant, Boy Kicking Box, *Halfway Up the Sky,* Abingdon Press, Nashville, Tennessee, 1985.

Chapter 3

MY SEARCH FOR HELP

After the docility which shock had produced in her yester-
day, he wasn't prepared for the change even though he
knew that her anger was natural, a need to strike out and
would so that someone, somehow, would feel some of her
pain [1, p. 254].

Elizabeth George

The intensity of my initial pain surprised me, and I often felt
the need to "strike out." My anger arose from the unfairness I
felt at the death of one so young as Alex. My relationship to
him had not only involved a special bonding, but the emotional
energy and hidden hopes of immortality I had invested in him.
Outliving my grandchild was an indescribable attack on the
very essence of my being.

How could I possibly process such sorrow? In what con-
ceivable way could I offer support to my grieving child and his
family? Were there answers to these questions?

FRIENDS AND FAMILY

The most obvious place to ask questions and seek support
would be from family and friends. Or so I thought. With
dismay, I quickly learned that family and friends found my
questions, and my need to talk about my grief, tedious and
tiring. One of my close friends hung up the phone on me one
day after indicating she did not wish to associate with me until

I had "gotten over it," I wrote her a long letter including a passage from "Please Listen."

> Listen! All I asked was that you listen, not talk, or do—
> just hear me . . . [2, p. 127].

I asked her to "forgive me for being irritable, irrational, angry, and weepy at times. I need your understanding, your patience, and your presence. Please don't offer me advice on 'how' I should be grieving; judgments of 'where' I am in the process; or 'what to do' to 'speed up' the process, and when I should be finished. If you don't know what to say, listen! Then, I will know you care."

Even my patient, kind, and loving husband grew weary of my distress. As David's stepfather, he probably did not have the same emotional attachment to Alex as I, nor did he have the same opportunity to get to know Alex as well as I did. He, like many, felt more comfortable offering advice rather than listening.

Fortunately I had established a relationship prior to Alex's death with a private therapist. That association proved to be of inestimable aid. Finding others who would tolerate my sorrowing soul for any length of time proved difficult.

GRIEF SUPPORT GROUPS

Upon returning home, I searched for a grief support group for myself. Numerous groups were available for parents, widows, and widowers, but none specifically for grandparents. The Compassionate Friends,[1] a national organization for grieving parents, has several active chapters in my area. TCF encourages grandparent participation in their groups. Other grandparents[2] felt as I did, that being there to support the grieving parents may be good, but the particular issues of grandparents would best be addressed in a separate group. No

---

[1] The Compassionate Friends, P.O. Box 3696, Oak Brook, IL 60522-3696.

[2] Through personal conversations and Grandparents Questionnaire.

such group existed in my community at that time. And I didn't feel I had the energy to start one.

A general grief group that met at a local senior center I found most beneficial, however. Prior to becoming a regular member of that group, however, I had visited several other grief support groups. Not all those experiences were supportive. One of the groups I attended met at an establishment that promotes itself as a caring and progressive institution. I cannot imagine how my reaction to that group could have been worse. At the time of my visit to this group, I had attended several other grief groups, and before Alex's death I had had considerable experience with both therapeutic and support groups. Small groups of five to ten people seemed to work best. The major benefit of such groups comes from allowing participants to tell their stories. Thus, grief groups allow members to experience what Kathryn Cramer claims is the value of allowing trauma to teach us through the expression of our stories, retelling and reflecting on them as often as we might be inclined to do so [3, p. 260].

Imagine my surprise then at one group I attended that had about twenty-five people and a female facilitator claiming to be a "certified" grief counselor, but who invariably interrupted, after only a few moments, the group members' stories. She then would proceed to lecture that individual on what he/she needed to do. By the time I was given an opportunity to speak, I realized the need for brevity. I was not brief enough. The facilitator interrupted me and offered the possibility that, "When we are dealing with a child, we can think that had he lived, he might have become crippled, or something else bad happen to him, so perhaps we can say it is just as well that he didn't live."

To say her words were not beneficial to me is to understate the obvious. During the meeting she had made it abundantly clear that she believed "life in heaven" was preferable to this earthly life, and that she knew for certain that her deceased husband was "in heaven and playing golf up there."

In a follow-up letter to her, I referred to Joseph Fischoff's comment, ". . . life with the child alive, even chronically ill or in pain, is better than not having the child at all" [4, p. 8]. I also stated my hurt and anger at her cruel remarks and my dismay that a certified grief counselor would be so insensitive. I told her that, "For myself (and I am absolutely certain, for others as well), this life is wonderful, joyous, and vitally important—particularly since in our human knowledge it is all we know for sure. And, my family and I would have liked to have had our little Alex with us for more of it."

As astonishing as I had found her statement, it was no more so than her non-response to my letter. When I had not received an acknowledgment after several weeks, I wrote another letter to the director of the program (a psychologist) and enclosed a copy of my original letter to the facilitator. Again there was no response. My need was not for them to concur with me, but simply to recognize my pain and distress; to hear me.

When I discussed the situation with other professionals in the field, I learned how frequently even professionals dismiss the comments of a grieving person. What a terrible lack of understanding and empathy, especially when the need for someone to listen is so critical.

Fortunately, there are groups and professionals who do understand the needs of the grieving. Finding the right ones sometimes requires persistence in locating them.

SEMINARS/LECTURES

While I mourned, I expanded my quest for information by taking as many opportunities as possible to learn about the grief process. New Song,[3] a local organization dealing with sibling grief, gave an eight-week training/information course I attended. Several seminars, including an excellent one given by Alan Wolfelt,[4] and one by Marilyn Gryte,[5] were extremely beneficial.

---

[3] New Song, 6947 E. McDonald Dr., Paradise Valley, AZ 85253 (602) 951-8985.

[4] Alan Wolfelt, Center for Loss & Life Transition, 3735 Broken Bow Road, Fort Collins, CO 80526.

[5] "When a Baby Dies, Helping Family Grieve," Marilyn Gryte, RN, MS, Lecturer, Carondelet Management Institute, Phoenix, AZ, September 17, 1992.

QUESTIONNAIRE

Wanting to understand what being a bereaved grand-parent meant to others, I developed a questionnaire. Professional associates, friends, and acquaintances alerted me to people they knew who had lost a grandchild, and many completed my survey. My small survey confirmed my belief that grandparents suffer a dual loss when a grandchild dies. Through their responses I gained support and comfort for my feelings, and an appreciation for the suffering of other grandparents.

Some of the surveys were sent and received via e-mail. There are a number of Internet[6] sites that deal with grief and some have special areas for grandparent's grief.

BOOKS AND ARTICLES

Always a voracious reader, I naturally turned to books for information about grandparents' grief. Finding useful information in grief literature specific to grandparents' grief proved to be a daunting task. Little attention has been given to the role of grandparents when a grandchild dies. That lack does not, I believe, reflect the reality of the grandparent/grandchild relationships; nor the subsequent grief on the loss of a grandchild.

There are numerous books by parents, or authors quoting parents, describing parents' feelings, and how they coped with the loss of a child [5]. I have read—and wept while doing so—many of those accounts. Those first-person stories helped me begin to understand some of David and Andrea's sorrow.

My search also located a number of books written about parental grief. *The Bereaved Parent* by Harriet Sarnoff Schiff is considered by many authorities to be the quint-essential book for grieving parents [6]. I anticipated finding information for grandparents in her subsequent book, *Living*

---

[6] See Appendix II, Resources.

Through Mourning: Finding Comfort and Hope When A Loved One Has Died [7]. She included in that book chapters for parents, widows, widowers, children, siblings, and friends, but none for grandparents. Another book by Sherry Johnson, with the seemingly-inclusive title *After a Child Dies: Counseling Bereaved Families,* does not even list grandparents in the index [8]. This, I discovered, was the norm. Those authors who do mention grandparents and the duality of their loss usually do so as a brief and peripheral note.

In her excellent and extensive discussion of parental loss, Therese A. Rando sums up her entire discussion of grandparents' grief in one paragraph. She mentions their importance in many families, and how difficult a grandparents' role, for "They not only lose their grandchild, but they 'lose' their child as well, as they cannot rescue their child from bereaved-parent status" [9].

I found only one author, James Ponzetti, who has studied the grandparents' place in the family grieving process. He validates the important role of grandparents by stating, "To overlook their function in the family grieving process is to ignore a vital element" [10]. It is unfortunate that the reports on his studies are sketchy and available only in professional journals.

Margaret H. Gerner's small pamphlet is the only publication I found that addressed the subject of grandparents' grief with any depth and understanding [11]. As a bereaved parent, and also a bereaved grandparent, Ms. Gerner writes with touching sensitivity about the subject of grandparents' grief. Her pamphlet, however, is not widely published nor readily available, and I spent considerable time and effort in locating it.

Only recently I found the book *Grandma's Tears,* by June Cerza Kolf [12]. Ms. Kolf has worked with the terminally ill and the bereaved for many years. She treats the subject of grandparents' grief with a brief and sympathetic approach although she herself has not experienced such a death.

Through my efforts to confront my grief, and the disappointment at finding little practical information, I came to understand some truths about those who grieve. Elizabeth George, in her novel *A Suitable Vengeance,* has her character speak one of those certainties:

> The worst part of a death was always that moment of knowing beyond a doubt that no matter how many people share it—be they family, friends, or even an entire nation—no two people can ever feel it the same way. So it always seems as if one experiences it alone [13, p. 254].

I felt alone in my grief. Taking Rando's suggestion that, "Many of the issues pertinent to bereaved parents are salient for bereaved grandparents" [9, p. 37], I searched for clues to some of my own and my children's needs, and began perusing many of numerous books available about the grief process. Some of the books are written in very simple language with good, clear suggestions, and are easy to read when our attention span is very short. Some books discuss grief from particular deaths and range from elegant personal stories to in-depth and academic studies.

I continue to read, study, and attend seminars about grief. My active involvement with those that grieve includes being a facilitator for a grief group, and writing this book. Those activities are, I believe, fitting ways of honoring Alex's memory.

REFERENCES

1. E. George, *A Suitable Vengeance,* Bantam Books, New York, 1991.
2. R. Houghton, Please Listen, as quoted in *The Promise of Green in the Season of Grief,* D. Roth (ed.), Riverrun Press, Piermont, New York, 1987. The citation in this book is said to have been copied from *Trinity Reformed Chimes,* but I have seen the poem quoted with some of the words different, and attributed to Ray Roughton, in *Beyond Sympathy* by J. Harris, Pathfinder, Ventura, California, 1988, and many other places as "anonymous."

3. K. Cramer, *Staying On Top When Your World Turns Upside Down*, Viking, New York, 1990.
4. J. Fischhoff and N. O'Brien Brohl, *Before And After My Child Died*, Emmons-Fairfield, Detroit, 1981.
5. Examples include: J. Bramblett, *When Good-Bye is Forever: Learning to Live Again After the Loss of a Child*, Ballantine Books, New York, 1991; B. D. Van Vechten, *The First Year of Forever: Surviving the Death of Our Son*, Atheneum, New York, 1982; and R. Knapp, *Beyond Endurance: When a Child Dies*, Schocken Books, New York, 1986.
6. H. S. Schiff, *The Bereaved Parent*, Penguin Books, New York, 1977.
7. H. S. Schiff, *Living Through Mourning: Finding Comfort and Hope When a Loved One Has Died*, Penguin Books, New York, 1987.
8. S. E. Johnson, *After a Child Dies: Counseling Bereaved Families*, Springer, New York, 1987.
9. T. A. Rando, *Parental Loss of a Child*, Research Press, Champaign, Illinois, 1986.
10. J. J. Ponzetti, Bereaved Families: A Comparison of Parents' and Grandparents' Reactions to the Death of a Child, *Omega: Journal of Death and Dying*, 25:1, pp. 63-71, 1992.
11. M. H. Gerner, *For Bereaved Grandparents*, The Centering Corporation, Omaha, Nebraska, 1990.
12. J. C. Kolf, *Grandma's Tears*, Baker Books, Grand Rapids, Michigan, 1995.
13. E. George, *A Suitable Vengeance*, Bantam Books, New York, 1993.

Chapter 4

THE GRIEF PROCESS

> Grief is a tidal wave that overtakes you, smashes down
> upon you with unimaginable force, sweeps you up into its
> darkness, where you tumble and crash against unidentifi-
> able surfaces, only to be thrown out on an unknown beach,
> bruised, reshaped [1, p. 7].
>
> *Stephanie Ericsson*

Potent, painful, and unfamiliar emotions battered me between
the "tidal wave" and the "reshaping." I thought I knew about
grief. I was wrong. The loss of numerous adults, including my
parents, brother, cousin, and several good friends had brought
grief and sadness, but most had lived long and fruitful lives.
Those deaths had a sense of completeness, a certain natural
order to their deaths. They did nothing to prepare me for the
death of my grandson.

My professional training and experience had strengthened
beliefs that cessation of our biological life is a given. Nonetheless, the moment Alex died, shock and numbness accompanied
my stunned disbelief. I balked, physically, mentally, and
spiritually; resisted that truth; screamed in pain; and
scavenged for ways to keep my precious grandson from having
vanished, leaving only wisps of memory. And the devastation
brought by Alex's death on his father and mother was more
than I thought I could bear. This, then, was grief as I had
never known it.

Our family learned quickly what Katherine Fair Donnelly
meant when she said, "The most difficult hurdle is the initial

attempt to re-enter the world that can never be the same" [2, p. 43]. My desperate heart and mind wanted things to be the same. They were not, never would be. Consequently, my thoughts and feelings often bordered on the incoherent and nonsensical. As I returned to Alex's grave one evening with water for flowers we had taken there earlier, a crazy thought assailed me. Stepping from the car into the damp, cold grass I thought, "it's cold out here, Alex will get cold."

One of my recurring crazy thoughts was an intermittent repetition in my head of "All the king's horses and all the king's men couldn't put Humpty Dumpty together again," as the horrible images of Alex's last days flashed through my memory. Some moments I felt, knew, that Alex had survived his terrible illness. Then followed the anger and anguish knowing he did not. My attempts to find some semblance of normality proved to be elusive because, as Ginny Cunningham states, "Each member of the family had been forcibly propelled from his or her place in one constellation and placed unexpectedly on a new and unfamiliar trajectory" [3, p. 26].

My new path felt scary, unacceptable, and very painful. The pain alerted me to the seriousness of the situation, a desperate plea from the center of my being to pay attention. Instinctively I knew I needed help, and I also wanted to help David, Andrea, and their surviving children to withstand this terrible wound.

What small amount of knowledge I thought I had about the grief process, and what I was learning from my subjective experience of Alex's death, felt inadequate. Unable to locate anything about grandparents' grief, I looked at general grief literature and that written by, about, and for bereaved parents, in the hope that some of that material would be transferable to grandparents' grief.

I discovered that some authorities distinguish between grief and mourning: grief being defined as the internal, searing sadness felt from loss; different from mourning which is described as, "a shared social response to grief" [4, p. 10].

Whatever the semantics, everyone agrees that grief brings sadness. Since sadness is painful, we try to avoid it, but holding onto the pain of grief will freeze the pain within us. Through the act of mourning, pain and sadness may be discharged so healing may begin. I have found often elegant references to this process in modern fiction, including Sara Paretsky's *Indemnity Only:*

> All mourning takes a long time, and you can't rush it along. My dad's been dead ten years now, and every now and then, something comes up that lets me know that the mourning is still going on, and another piece of it is in place. The hard part doesn't last so long. While it is going on, though, don't fight it—the more you poke away the grief and anger, the longer it takes to sort it out" [5, p. 270].

Sara Paretsky's "hard part" may not have lasted very long, but mine felt like it did. There were moments, days, and even weeks when I thought I would not survive, much less enjoy life again. Those effects were the result of my loss, a word that suggests damage, dispossession, even possible extinction.

My loss of Alex felt overwhelming, and witnessing David and Andrea's suffering increased that sense of devastation. The description of the terrible reality of a child's death for parents is succinctly described by Ronald Knapp in his book *Beyond Endurance: When A Child Dies.* He says that, "In many ways the death of a child represents in a symbolic way the death of the self. Symbolically, a mother or father will die along with the child, only to survive in a damaged state with little or no desire to live today or plan for tomorrow" [6, p. 13].

David and Andrea had suffered a damaging wound and it hurt me terribly to watch, to listen to, and to be aware of their tremendous struggle to survive this blow. Although I had spent considerable time with them and their family and always enjoyed their company, now I felt at a loss as to how to relate to them. Our entire family had been affected psychologically, socially, and physically.

PHYSICAL NEEDS

Undue stress, from both recent happy events and from my grief, made for enormous claims on my physical health. I knew that my physical needs included:

- *Rest.* Although very much aware of the need for extra rest I often found my fatigue to be extreme and surprising, and needed to remind myself to rest.
- *Sleep.* The ability to go to sleep and to remain asleep was sometimes troublesome, but I knew this was not the time for drugs or alcohol, and would either get up and read or do meditation while resting.
- *Diet.* Rarely in my life have I failed to have the desire to eat, and yet many times I had to remind myself to eat properly.
- *Exercise.* I am by nature a very physical person, so hiking, playing tennis, and gardening were useful means of exercise for me. When I was feeling very depressed, I could usually muster up the energy to do some physical exercise which always made me feel better.
- *Activities.* Some of my physical responses were of the mildly violent nature, such as hitting walls with my fists. Other physical activities that helped, especially during periods of anger and irritability, included listening to music and working with clay.
- *Touch.* Hugs and stroking of the skin have great healing power. When traditional touching such as hugs and being held were not available, swimming gave me a needed sense of touch, as did regular massages. They were often part of my "personal care" days that included a manicure, bubble bath, and other be-good-to-myself activities.
- *Crying.* I knew that the different chemical component of tears from sadness indicates the healing properties of crying.[1] It was with great effort, however, that I learned to

---

[1] http.www.geisinger.edu/ghs/pubtips/P/THEPURPOSEOFTEARS.htm

allow my tears to flow freely, especially when they came unbidden, at unexpected times.

Just trying to care for myself was exhausting as I struggled with my own physical and emotional upheavals that often came in waves, making daily life seemingly infinitely difficult. Tears and constricted breathing were frequent; exhaustion seemed to be the norm. The need for my son to have knee surgery, my own oral surgery within a few months following Alex's death, and, later, Andrea's surgery for an ectopic pregnancy only added to our physical distress.[2] We all suffered from frequent cold and flu symptoms and the aches and pains from minor accidents and injuries caused by our inattention and weariness.

Weight gain or loss are typical physical problems following loss. One of my traditional methods of comforting myself is eating, especially frozen yogurt, so I gained ten pounds after Alex died. Andrea shares my proclivity to eat when under stress, with the same results. Besides the frequent crying and constant fatigue, her most profound physical distress was heart palpitations. She would often call me when experiencing those frightful symptoms. Sometimes I would be struggling in the pit of my sorrow when she called, and sometimes I would be having a short period of near-normalcy. No matter where I was emotionally, the harsh reality of her suffering always affected me. My heart would go out to her in her terrible distress, and my frustration at my inability to take away her pain always increased.

As profoundly injured as if from a physical injury, we required healing. A common cliché, "time will heal," alludes to the belief that the pain of grief declines steadily over time. Grief's healing process, however, is quite different from the steady cellular restoration associated with physical healing.

The suffering from the loss of a child feels more like an amputation than a bruise. Such trauma requires adaptation

---

[2] A year after Alex's death, Curtis developed a life-threatening illness, due to the same genetic defect, adding even more adversity (see Epilogue).

to an irretrievable loss, experienced not so much like healing as the gradual acceptance of a pain. Pain as Therese Rando describes as something:

> ... that fluctuates episodically in intensity and changes in complexion over time, but does not necessarily diminish, and never disappears. As one adapts to the loss of a limb, so one adapts to the loss of a child, but there is no restoration to a point of prior normalcy. One can no more alter the status of being a bereaved parent (or grandparent) than one can reverse the aging process; the rest of one's life is indelibly defined by a condition for which there is neither a reversal nor an adequate prosthesis [7, p. 417].

Now indelibly defined as a bereaved grandparent, I struggled to accept what had transpired, aware that my family's life had changed radically. Our relationships, and approaches to life, would need to undergo enormous transformation. To recover from the damage of Alex's death required, we soon discovered, enormous amounts of time. We were frequently dismayed by the time and energy our grief demanded and quickly learned that, although all who mourn share common characteristics, nothing about grieving is normal.

THE STAGES/PHASES

Since Elisabeth Kübler-Ross first opened the discussion on grief and suggested specific "stages" of grief, other students of bereavement have modified these original stages or developed new models of the grief process [8]. It is now possible to find many different ideas regarding the number and types of stages, phases, of grief and their order.

These various "stages" of mourning are not experienced by all, nor are they distinct and orderly. They are often experienced as fluctuating back and forth or together, and in varying intensity or not at all, depending on the individual. Some simplified descriptions of the grief process arrange the most prevalent experiences and behaviors into phases of bereavement such as:

1. Shock and Numbness
   Stunned feelings, disbelief, denial, time confusion,
   failure to accept reality
   Short attention span, difficulty in concentrating and
   making decisions
   Resistance to stimuli, poor functioning

2. Searching and Yearning
   Anger, guilt, bargaining
   Restlessness, sensitive to stimuli, irritability
   Sleep disturbances, insomnia, headaches, lack of
   strength
   Palpitation, aching arms, sighing
   Resentment, bitterness, preoccupation with the
   deceased

3. Disorientation
   "Crazy" thoughts, forgetfulness, social withdrawal
   Sadness, exhaustion, lack of energy, insomnia
   Depression, difficulty in concentrating, guilt feelings,
   sense of failure
   Anorexia or weight gain, feelings of illness

4. Reorganization/Resolution
   Better able to make decisions
   Renewed energy, able to laugh and smile
   Eating and sleeping habits improved
   Sense of release, planning for the future

One of the models of mourning I found cited frequently is
Worden's "Tasks of Mourning":

1. Accept the reality of the loss.
2. Experience the pain of grief.
3. Adjust to an environment without that which has been
   lost.
4. Withdrawing emotional energy and reinvesting it in
   another relationship [9].

Worden's model, and other common models, Therese Rando alleges, are inadequate for parental bereavement. She believes that many of the psychological and social variables usually considered contributors to the diagnosis of "failure to grieve" are commonly prevalent in parental bereavement [7, pp. 47-55].

Worden's first task, accepting the reality of the loss, is very difficult for parents, Rando claims, because it "violates one of the basic functions of being an adult, defies the laws of nature and orderliness of the universe, multiply victimizes the parents, and savagely assaults their sense of self and their abilities" [7, p. 47].

I doubted my ability to cope and feared making poor judgments. David and Andrea expressed similar apprehensions. Despite desperate efforts to stay in control, emotional swings became part of our daily lives. Our unfocused anxiety showed itself in seemingly unrelenting restlessness and tension. Often four strong emotions—fear, sadness, anger, and guilt—intertwined in endless and often troubling patterns. All spilled forth at unexpected times; life seemed hollow and despair unending.

Frustration and insecurity occasionally rational, but more often totally illogical, aggravated my feelings of anger and guilt. My rejection of reality often took the form of a constant thought, "This cannot be." Our society, with its tremendous faith in medical science, encourages the denial of childhood death. I was not immune to either that faith, nor to that subsequent denial.

Frequently, thoughts crept into my mind about how we could have done things differently, such as "If I had stayed longer, if I had just gone over sooner, if this, if that." Although my rational mind knew nothing would have altered the outcome, my heart had difficulty acknowledging and accepting what had befallen our family.

Worden's second task, experiencing the pain of grief, is exaggerated for bereaved parents (and grandparents). It is not just the loss of a relationship that creates the pain of grief Rando states, but the loss of hopes and dreams—parts of themselves and their immortality represented by the child. Rando's position is that the loss of those parts of self are so excruciating that "the premature separation from one's child would be expected to generate the most severe torment possible" [7, p. 48].

Torment is a good description of our life following Alex's death. We did not, however, attempt to "just get over it," or try to will away the terrible void of loss by keeping busy. According to many authorities, these characteristics and patterns can lead to problems so critical, according to James Ponzetti, that the "failure to grieve both as an individual and as a whole family can lead to serious dysfunction" [10, p. 64].

With great difficulty we chose to face, talk about, and share our pain. We endeavored to grieve both independently and collectively. Individually we processed our grief in the manner that best suited us, and we made special time to stop and mourn together as a family. The pull of sympathy for others in the family often made it difficult to balance those needs with the egotistical task of one's own mourning. If temporarily one of us had found a resting place in our grief, another member's profound sense of grief at that particular time could dissolve that short period of tranquillity.

Making the effort to process and therefore experience the pain of my grief seemed imperative. It was not easy to do. I often felt confused. My attention span was short, energy level at a low ebb and my interests extremely narrow. I withdrew from several of my normal activities, including church choir (after 25 years), as I found it difficult to concentrate and attending often increased my irritability. My method of functioning in and relating to the world included a lack of concentration and interest in daily life; behavior that felt scary to me and disconcerting to family and friends.

It also included many of the other usual reactions to loss:

- A sense of powerlessness/frustration.
  I could not change what had happened.

- Obsessive preoccupation with loss.
  The frequent need to talk about Alex's death did not
  endear me to friends.
- An inability to concentrate.
  Ordinary activities became difficult to accomplish.
- Deflective thinking/talking.
  The minutiae of weather, news, and sports were easier to
  think about and discuss than my grief.
- Loneliness/depression/ambivalence.
  Family, friends, and even sometimes clergy and
  counselors, supportive during the early weeks or months,
  soon suggested "It is time to get over it."
- Bitterness/resentment.
- Questioning of why it had to happen.
- And always, the fatigue and sadness.

One formidable dilemma, particularly for bereaved
parents, that holds true for grandparents as well, is the
unevenness of the grief experience. Everyone's grief is unique.
We grieve in our own way and time, and the triggers to each
person's grief are different. Members of my family soon
became aware of periods when an individual family member's
emotions were quite unlike those of the others.

One factor contributing to this problem for parents is if
the mother remains at home with surviving children, like
Andrea. In such a capacity, she was constantly reminded
of her loss; her husband, however, was in a different
environment at his workplace. As a result, even such small
decisions as to what clothes and toys of Alex's would be made
available for Stephanie became problematic for David and
Andrea.

Recent studies have indicated, contrary to what might be
expected, that the grief of mothers may be more intense after
two years. The ramifications of this phenomenon means that the
anger for mothers may be more difficult after two years after
death when most social support is withdrawn and their own
husbands are suffering much less intensely [7, p. 417]. Even
after five years, the measures of intensity diminish to levels

only slightly below those of the first two years, while fathers show a steady decrease in their intensity of grief after two and five years [7, p. 417]. Mothers tend to have significantly higher levels of anger, guilt, and social isolation.

Many of these same characteristics probably exist for grandmothers as well. Certainly my sense of outrage and anger has continued beyond everyone's sympathy and support. More than once in recent years my husband has commented that I have not "dealt very well with Alex's death." He says he does not "agree with" the manner in which David, Andrea, and myself "handle our grief."

These unpredictable and intense factors of grief discrepancy create the frequently cited serious marital difficulties following the death of a child. Other than my personal experience, I have no information regarding marital problems or strains on grandmother/grandfather relationships following the death of a grandchild. It never occurred to me at the time to include such a question on the survey I developed to query grandparents about their feelings and experiences following the death of a grandchild. Only later did I find information that estimated as many as 75 to 90 percent of bereaved couples may divorce if professional help is not sought [7, p. 416]. The chaplain at the hospital warned David and Andrea of that statistic almost immediately following Alex's death. We felt it was an inappropriate subject for the time, but it was good and accurate advice.

Worden's third task, adjusting to the environment without that which has been lost, presents a terrible dilemma for many parents as it often requires parents to function in the same environment, performing the same roles, for surviving children. Parents cannot simply stop being parents. If there are other children, the bereaved parent must continue his or her parental interaction and parenting. The same is true for grandparents. Often there are other grandchildren who need love and attention from the grandparents who may find it difficult to give as they struggle with their grief. And then there may be surviving children in the family that are grieving, as there were in ours.

Curtis, at age eight, certainly felt the effects of his brother's death, and he was old enough to verbalize his distress, to ask questions, and to comfort or distract himself at times. That was not the case for Stephanie. She was just six weeks old when Alex died. David and Andrea questioned their ability to care properly for their newborn daughter. I believe Stephanie's incredible personality and even temperament helped her parents, and all of us. As she did at the hospital, her very presence gave us all nourishing love. The physical and emotional benefits of a beloved newborn were incomparable.

Worden's fourth task, withdrawing emotional energy and reinvesting it in another relationship, is the most controversial. Rando claims, "it is terribly difficult because it requires parents to attempt mutually incompatible tasks, simultaneously holding on and letting go" [7, p. 49]. Furthermore, the child has been invested with myriad symbolic meaning; the hopes, dreams, needs, and wishes for immortality, and now the parents, and grandparents, are faced with the need to let go of those aspects of the self while retaining some of them at the same time. "Would that a parent's grief could be buried with the child" [2, p. 43]. It cannot, of course, neither for a parent nor for a grandparent.

For those of us who take issue with Worden's fourth task, the controversy is probably more one of the use of terms, rather than actuality. Somehow the words "withdrawing" and "reinvesting" strike a chord of disloyalty. Rather, the idea of release, reconciliation, and reorganization carries a more agreeable connotation. Reconciliation allows a new harmony to develop in our lives without Alex, while retaining and honoring the memory of him. In that way the important aspects of his personality (his loving nature and joy of life) may be held in our hearts and incorporated into our lives. Through our mourning we have developed a new relationship with Alex and, subsequently, new identities for ourselves.

REFERENCES

1. S. Ericsson, *Companion Through the Darkness: Inner Dialogues on Grief,* Harper Perennial, New York, 1993.
2. K. F. Donnelly, *Recovering from the Loss of a Child,* Macmillan, New York, p. 43, 1982.
3. G. Cunningham, How to Pay Your Respects to Grief, *U.S. Catholic,* July 1994.
4. A. Wolfelt, *Helping Children Cope with Grief,* Accelerated Development, Inc., Muncie, Indiana, p. 10, 1983.
5. S. Paretsky, *Indemnity Only,* Dell, New York, p. 270, 1992.
6. R. Knapp, *Beyond Endurance: When a Child Dies,* Schocken Books, New York, 1986.
7. T. A. Rando (ed.), *Parental Loss of a Child,* Research Press Company, Champaign, Illinois, 1986.
8. E. Kübler-Ross, *On Death and Dying,* Macmillan, New York, 1969.
9. W. Worden, *Grief Counseling and Grief Therapy: A Handbook for the Mental Health Practitioner,* Springer, New York, 1982.
10. J. J. Ponzetti, Bereaved Families: A Comparison of Parents' and Grandparents' Reactions to the Death of a Child, *Omega: Journal of Death and Dying,* 25:1, p. 64, 1992.

Chapter 5

HELPING MYSELF

Time itself doesn't heal. It only gives us room to free ourselves, and the opportunity to heal ourselves of past wounds. Time offers us the eternal present of possibility. We determine that possibility [1, p. 176].

Alla Renee Bozarth

With time, we can heal ourselves and determine the "possibility" of our lives. Others may surround and support us, yet the ultimate responsibility for the shape of our lives following the death of a loved one rests with us—a difficult and consuming task. But we are the only ones who can determine how we manage our grief.

Whether we grieve as a grandmother or grandfather, whether our loss is single or multiple, whether due to illness, accident, suicide, or murder, we must all cope with the shock to our physical, psychological, social, and spiritual lives. What we do with that shock, the decisions we make, will determine much about our future.

Most of society's support has gone, and rightly so, to the parents when a child dies. However, the death of a child also has enormous consequences for the entire family, causing "an 'emotional shock wave' that can shake the extended family system's equilibrium for years afterwards . . ." [2, p. 36]. A significant part of the "extended family system" is the grandparent/grandchild relationship. If we have a grandchild die, we will experience that "shock wave." Only by taking care of ourselves, helping ourselves, will we be able to survive and regain the possibility for our lives.

PAIN AND CRYING

First comes the pain. Pain follows any wounding. Immediate and frightening, pain functions as a physical and psychic message to us. Wounds require attention. A spiritual/psychic wound needs loving care just as surely as a physical wound.

A natural response to pain, crying, is, Bozarth says, ". . . what you do when you can't do anything else . . ." [1, p. 54]. The tears of grief contain chemicals that are different from those of regular tears.[1] Crying can be considered a method of flushing away the toxic residue of grief. Giving ourselves permission to cry releases stress and tension, physically and emotionally.

For some of us, and perhaps for all of us at certain times, it may be necessary to find a safe place to cry, one where we will not be interrupted or ridiculed. Driving a car while crying, I've found, is not a good idea (good time to scream, however, if the windows are rolled up), but the shower is a greater place to cry. If we try to hold back our tears by tightening our facial and throat muscles, we only add to our distress. We may postpone for a little time the release of our feelings, but any attempts to suffocate them will only create more physical and emotional agony.

WRITING

Pain, anger, and confusion look different, and often less overwhelming on paper. Driving and crying may not be a good idea, but I discovered I could write and cry at the same time, and that often the two of them together were somehow even more useful. My early journal writing after Alex's death looked pretty much like I felt, incoherent and weepy. Often heavy slashes from my pen or pencil gave evidence of my

---

[1] http.www.geisinger.edu/ghs/pubtips/P/THEPURPOSEOFTEARS.htm

anger, but sometimes after journaling my grief looked and felt temporarily manageable.

Writing in a journal (any old notebook will do) is an excellent way to help process our grief. As one of my correspondents stated, "I thought I was doing pretty good until I started to put all of this on paper."[2] We need not be a "writer" to use that method for expressing our pain. By writing our thoughts and feelings on paper we may get in touch with hidden factors of our grief, and thus gain some control over the uncomfortable and unacknowledged elements of our pain. Through the "naming" of our pain and fears we can help ourselves heal. Gabriele Rico, in *Pain and Possibility*, states that, "The very act of putting pencil to paper is an act of giving shape to amorphous feelings. The act of writing helps name the unnameable: the chaotic feelings we resist, fear or remain unaware of" [3, p. 2].

Writing in a journal has become a regular habit for me. Such activity allows me to support myself in a private, always available manner. It allows a full expression of feelings without concern for embarrassment or censure. The process of writing, scribbling, or just doodling, assists me in releasing pain and clarifying my thoughts and feelings.

EVALUATING MY STRENGTHS

Taking an accounting of my strengths helped me through my grieving. Many of the other grandparents with whom I have corresponded mention using their particular knowledge and strengths as invaluable to them during their mourning.[3]

I had always considered myself to be a "survivor," but after Alex's death I questioned that ability. As has been my habit, I read books to find something to bolster my sagging confidence. In Frederic Flach's book *Resilience*, I found a description of a resilient personality: someone with the insight or motivation

---

[2] Personal correspondence.

[3] Personal correspondence.

to reach out for guidance, know he is in trouble, and seek help from someone [4, p. 111]. Other attributes of a resilient personality that the author mentioned that I felt I possessed included:

- Independence of thought and action without fear of relying on others, or reluctance to do so.
- A high level of personal discipline and sense of responsibility.
- A keen sense of humor.
- A high tolerance of distress.
- Insight into one's own feelings and those of others, and the ability to communicate these in an appropriate manner.
- Focus, a commitment to life, and a philosophical framework within which personal experiences can be interpreted with meaning and hope, even at life's seemingly most hopeless moments [4, pp. 113-114].

Identifying those parts of my personality that indicated a resilient individual increased my courage to face my grief.

PERSONAL TIMELINE

Through the act of reviewing my strengths, I gained strength. Looking at how past losses had affected my current loss helped me gain insight into my feelings. I developed a timeline of significant events in my life. The following is a simplified version (starting with first memory) of major events in my life. In this example, lines above the horizontal line represent happy memories, lines below as unhappy, and the length denotes the remembered intensity (see Figure 1).

This exercise revealed enormous changes in my life between 1980 and 1990. The five grandchildren born during that decade significantly changed the configuration of my family, as did the deaths of important adults before and after Alex's death. Any change, good or bad, precipitates stress. The five happy births and the seven sad deaths in that decade had left me little time to assimilate any of them.

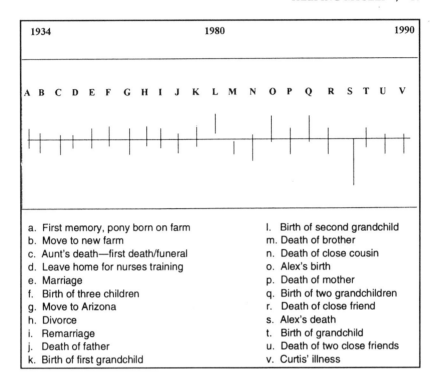

Figure 1. Simplified version of major events.

To heal, to regain some balance, I needed to finish mourning these past deaths, as well as Alex's. Unprocessed grief always depletes. Old losses impact new losses. For those of us who experienced the loss of a grandchild, I believe we need to examine what other previous losses we have had and how well we have processed those losses. We may need to re-examine our beliefs, values, strengths, and grieving methods.

Now I know that fully-experienced grief holds the potential for enriching our creativity and sensitivity. I didn't believe or even want to hear that right after Alex died. It would be some time into my grief journey before I could accept that potential. Caring for myself physically, emotionally, and spiritually came first.

PHYSICAL NEEDS

Nutrition

Although when we grieve we often forget about a well-balanced diet and an adequate fluid intake, they are vitally important in taking care of our shocked bodies. Although I knew how imperative it was to remember to care for my physical health, and that it was one aspect of my life that was under my control, it was still difficult. When we feel empty we usually either try to fill the void or not eat at all. Indulging in "comfort foods" from time to time can be beneficial, but I also knew the importance of striving to:

- Eat small amounts every two to three hours to reduce the stress of trying to assimilate large amounts of food. Frequent, small meals help stabilize our blood sugar at a time in our life when there is a tremendous drain on our physical resources.
- Eat healthy, well-balanced meals of grains, fresh fruits, and vegetables, with only small amounts of meat, dairy products, and fish. Fats and sweets need to be limited.
- Drink at least eight medium-sized glasses of water a day. A good way of making sure of adequate water intake may be to pour eight glasses of water in a pitcher every day and then make sure we drink it all during that day.
- Avoid caffeine, alcohol, and drugs. Dulling the pain with these only puts added strain on the body at a time when we are the least physically resilient.

Exercise

The body requires regular movement to maintain its optimum state. More often than not the fatigue of grief makes it difficult to do the exercising that can assist in withstanding the assault on our bodies and minds. I needed to remind myself:

- To gain energy, it is necessary to expend energy. Even mild exercise will help us feel more comfortable and energized.
- Regular exercise helps to relieve the depressive feelings of mourning.
- Physically-demanding exercise can assist in the relief of frustration and anger.
- If not accustomed to regular exercise, stretching (watch a cat!) and walking around the block several times a day is a good place to start.

Sleep/Relaxation

Sleep often eludes us during mourning, or we sleep more than usual. Quiet rest and relaxation can be almost as restorative as deep sleep. Some methods for relaxing and inducing sleep include:

- Deep breathing. We can become conscious of our breathing and then take deep, regular breaths.
- Practicing Yoga, Tai Chi, and/or meditation of any type.
- Daily exercise, which promotes restful sleep.
- Visualizing. (I like to imagine a serene, beautiful, enchanting place. In my mind, I experience the sights, sounds, smells, and the warmth or coolness of the place.)
- Routines of reading, listening to favorite music, bubble baths, and other personal relaxing activities all assist in relaxation and sleep.

Body Awareness

Our bodies reflect our emotions through posture and expression. By consciously choosing to be aware of our body we can help change our moods by:

- Cultivating a positive posture to improve breathing and a sense of well-being.

- Stretching our jaws. This action helps to produce relaxation and encourages deep breathing and yawning which will also improve our facial expression and feelings.
- Taking the time and making the effort to attend to our daily personal care and looking our best.
- Dressing in clothes that are comfortable and affect us positively.

PRIORITIZING

Grieving is exhausting business. To make the time necessary for bereavement, we need to:

- Simply stop unnecessary activities, let go of projects that are no longer important.
- Delegate, when possible, duties and responsibilities that feel overwhelming, but need doing.
- Let go of "friends" who suck the life force out of us—those that make cruel and thoughtless comments, who do not listen, who constantly "need" us.
- Not allow others to dictate what they think is best for us.
- Decline any new responsibilities until ready.
- Find those activities, friends, habits that comfort and support us.

SPIRITUALITY/RELIGION

If our religious faith sustains and support us, we can use it on a daily basis for meditation and comfort. I believe our personal sincerity is what matters with prayer and meditation, not what religious tradition we might embrace.

Spirituality with or without religious connections, however, can assist us in developing a sense of peace and contentment. One definition of spirituality that makes sense for me is ". . . a transcendental belief system through which we try to explain life" [5, p. 1]. A belief system that locates our beings as an essential part of the world, a part of a living network that connects every living thing, can give us strength and courage.

We can enhance our well-being and cultivate our religious and spiritual feelings through:

- Trusting our inner selves (intuition) to know what is right for us.
- Recognizing and appreciating the awe and wonder of each day.
- Creating order and elegance in our days.
- Identifying passions, interests, and hobbies that feed our soul.

1. Reading. Returning to old favorites and discovering new writings can bring us solace. (Libraries are a wonderful place to hide.)
2. Art. (The appreciation of looking at fine art, or actively engaging in some type of art activity such as painting or clay modeling, will help lighten our load of grief.)
3. Drawing. (Scribbles and doodles help us to expend anger and tension.)
4. Music. (Listening to favorites, or playing even the simplest of instruments, can increase our sense of freedom.)
5. Dancing. (Just allowing ourselves, in the privacy of our own homes, to move about in rhythm to music lifts tension and is an excellent exercise.)
6. Singing. (Loudly, especially, will increase breathing and our sense of well-being.)
7. Gardening. (The healing benefits of fresh air, sunshine, and earth are available to us in even the smallest of gardens.)
8. Walking, going fishing, visiting a zoo, sitting in a pretty park.
9. Movies, particularly favorite comedies, offer a respite from our grief, and laughter increases circulation and deep breathing.
10. Private rituals. A few minutes each day dedicated to: remembering, reading special poems or religious material, lighting a candle, putting a flower in a special vase—anything that memorializes the lost loved

one is a ritual act. These rituals help restore structure and meaning to our lives.

SOCIAL/EMOTIONAL SUPPORT

Any social support we have prior to a loss usually benefits us following that loss. Women generally, but not necessarily, have more social support than men. Because men often lack confidants, and grandfathers are often retired, it is doubly important for them to find social and emotional support in other ways. Men are usually the most resistant to attending grief groups and seeking individual therapy; perhaps our culture has asked them to bear the burden of "being strong" and "being the protector." Our culture encourages grandfathers to work through their grief process through different activities (such as work and sports) than those of grandmothers. They still need social and emotional support from family, friends, and associates.

Men and women may discover that our former social contacts no longer suffice in this new and different emotional situation. Usually it becomes self-evident who are able to be supportive to us through our grief journey. If it becomes obvious that we don't have a supportive person or persons within our family, church, or social circle, it is imperative then to seek out help either with professional assistance or a grief support group.

ASKING FOR HELP

Our emotional needs may be so great, or our personal and social resources so slim, that new support must be sought through:

- Asking for help from family, friends, and neighbors. Clear communications are essential; no one can read our minds. Ask for specific practical, physical help such as grocery shopping or yard work. Ask for specific time to be alone and also when we need companionship.
- Participation in grief groups. Groups differ, therefore it may be necessary to visit several before finding one that

fits our needs. Not all groups have trained facilitators, but the people in the best groups understand and tolerate the necessity of long-term discussion of our grief.
• Private counseling. The support and guidance of a professional at a time like this can be invaluable.

EDUCATING OURSELVES

Gaining information about grief and learning what others have experienced will help us know we are not alone and definitely not abnormal. We may feel our grief is unique (and it is to us), but others have suffered and studied grief and their knowledge will aid us in caring for ourselves during our bereavement. We can find information from:

• Books, articles, and videos which are readily available at libraries and bookstores. Many other institutions, such as hospitals and funeral homes, also offer useful information through pamphlets.
• Grief lectures, seminars, and study groups that are often sponsored by hospitals, hospices, community colleges, and sometimes funeral homes.
• Local, state, and national organizations that deal with death due to loss from miscarriage, stillbirth, newborn death, sudden infant death, specific illnesses (particularly cancer), accidents (motor vehicle especially), suicide, and murder.

By becoming involved with an organization of our choosing we can direct our energies in a positive and beneficial manner. As we learn more about the universality of death and how others have coped with loss, we can gain insight and understanding into our own needs, and thus help ourselves, help our child, and open up new possibilities for our lives.

REFERENCES

1. A. R. Bozarth, *Life is Goodbye, Life is Hello,* ComCare Publisher, Minneapolis, Minnesota, 1982.

2. T. A. Rando (ed.), *Parental Loss of a Child,* Research Press Company, Champaign, Illinois, 1986.
3. G. Rico, *Pain and Possibility: Writing Your Way Through Personal Crisis,* J. P. Tarcher Inc., Los Angeles, California, 1991.
4. F. Flach, *Resilience,* Fawcett Columbine, New York, 1988.
5. R. Elkins, Belief and Grief, (Gannett News Service), *Mesa Tribune,* Section F, September 26, 1998.

Chapter 6

HELPING OUR GRIEVING CHILD

I am powerlessness, I am helplessness.
I am frustration. I sit with her and I cry with her
I can't reach inside her and take her broken heart.
I must watch her suffer day after day [1].

Margaret H. Gerner

We cannot fix our grieving child's broken heart. Our first response when our child is injured, is to comfort. When a grandchild dies, we cannot take away our child's terrible anguish. We feel powerless and helpless.

Waiting until we recover from our own grief to find ways to help our child is not an option. Experiencing our own grief while simultaneously aiding our bereaved child characterizes grandparents' grief. Seeing the suffering of my child and his spouse compounded my distress from Alex's death, and I felt ill-prepared for the task ahead.

The exact manner in which we help our child will be as diverse as our relationships. The type and amount of assistance given will vary according to many factors, including the circumstances of the death and the health and personal and financial resources of the parties involved.

Some of us may have the privilege of being with our child and family through the initial crisis. We may, as I was, be with them at the time of death. When Alex was first admitted to the hospital around 1 P.M., David had called me. I suggested I fly over. He said to wait. Later that afternoon when Alex's

condition was diagnosed as critical and he was being transferred to another hospital, David called and said, "I need you
now." I took the first flight I could catch and arrived at the
hospital around 11 P.M. that evening.

Since I had been "mom" to both David and Andrea for
some time, I considered each of them to be my child, and
wished to give whatever help I could. Since I had the financial
ability and the personal time flexibility to be almost immediately available to them, I went to them and remained
with them throughout Alex's hospitalization. I tried my best to
be present for them and to give them my love and support
despite the potential pitfalls of such a task. I stayed with Alex
the first night he was in the hospital, and then through the
next day as David and Andrea got some much needed rest, and
returned to their home for clothes and supplies for us and
Stephanie.[1]

By the time I next slept, I had been awake for thirty-six
hours. The disorientation that I felt from my lack of sleep
during that time period was just the beginning of the emotional toll on all of us with a roller coaster of emotions and
eventually the searing moment of Alex's death. By the time the
funeral was over, I had been gone from my home for almost a
month. I felt mentally, emotionally, and physically exhausted.
I felt I needed to return home and regroup if I was to have any
hope of helping anyone.

Before I went home, however, I realized that immediate
and long-term emotional support would be essential for all of
us. David and Andrea were relatively new to their neighbor-
hood, and consequently had a limited circle of social and supportive resources. I encouraged them to attend a grief group
almost immediately after Alex's death, even before his funeral.
Several people have questioned that advice with, "Don't you
think that was too early?" Somehow I fail to understand how it
can ever be "too early" to reach out for assistance in a crisis.

---

[1] Because Andrea was breast-feeding Stephanie (and we really had no one to care
for her), we kept her at the hospital with us for the two-and-a-half weeks Alex was
hospitalized.

They did go to that meeting, and the group and members from the group proved to be of invaluable help to them.

No matter what the factors are regarding our grandchild's death, we will want to mend the wounds done to our child. We will want to protect, give perfect answers, fix the problem, and to make everything right again. That is not possible. What are we to do?

PHYSICAL/PRACTICAL

What we do will depend, of course, on each particular situation. Immediately before or after death we may have the opportunity, if we live nearby or as in my situation, to be with them to help with practical needs. We can help by running errands, taking care of their home, cooking meals, greeting guests, and if there are other children, caring for them. The fatigue of grief is physically and emotionally debilitating. We can ease some of that burden through practical help, but ask first. Some of the tasks they may prefer to do themselves or to leave undone.

I had spent considerable time in David and Andrea's home and felt comfortable doing many routine chores immediately after Alex's death. I tried to take care of baby Stephanie and nine-year-old Curtis' immediate needs. Sometimes there were specific chores that David and Andrea asked me to do, such as pressing the clothes they had chosen for Alex to be buried in as that felt too overwhelming for Andrea. I felt privileged to be asked to do that.

For most relationships, our physical presence is critical, and just being there can be of enormous significance, despite the difficulty of doing so. To cope with our grief, and yet contain it, while being available and supportive to our grieving child in as non-judgmental a manner as possible requires tremendous effort and sensibility.

I believe that, despite our personal beliefs and preferences, it is of paramount importance that our child's and his or her spouse's wishes for last rites for their child be honored. Those decisions may go against everything we cherish, and therefore will be a challenge to our ability to be non-judgmental and supportive.

TOUCH

As adults, we rarely admit we would like to be held. Following the death of a loved one, that need may be especially strong. While holding our child on our lap may not be either physically or emotionally imaginable, symbolically that type of comfort can be given through the magic of touch.

For sons as well as daughters, the touch of a held hand or an arm around the shoulder will convey comfort, love, and support. For those families (mine is one, thank goodness) that are comfortable with hugging, that action, that holding, can be caring and supportive for both participants.

ROLE MODELS

Whether intentionally or not, we function as role models for our grieving child. Our manner of mourning before and at the time of our grandchild's death, and through the long years of the bereavement to come, may profoundly influence our child's method of grieving. We have the opportunity, in our sorrow, to show, through our words and behavior, that it is possible to survive such an injury. Sharing our feelings of confusion and not having an answer for why this happened can help promote understanding between ourselves and our child and help assure them that they are not alone in their daze.

We can convey that "doing well" does not mean keeping our feelings inside, not talking about the loss of our loved one, and not crying. We can discuss and demonstrate that suppressed grief is unhealthy, both emotionally and physically.

If we have been taught (and still believe) that we need to "control" ourselves and still feel the need to pass that on to our bereaved children, we can, at the very least, restrain ourselves and allow them to find their own method of grieving.

LISTEN

We can encourage our child and spouse to talk, for to be heard is absolutely essential for bereaved parents. Someone who will listen may be the greatest gift we can give them. And it may be the most difficult thing we ever do. Listening completely and compassionately will require all of our strength and patience. Their agony will exacerbate our pain, and we must prepare ourselves for that added grief and somehow tolerate it.

The bereaved parents may shout their wrath against God, the medical establishment (physicians and others), and their own (perceived) weaknesses. If our child questions his faith, beliefs, or values (the ones we taught him), our capacity for tolerance may be severely tested. Both parents may express their anger and sense of failure in protecting their child, particularly in the case of accidents or murder, and their inability to help their child in the case of suicide. Their need to be heard is predominant, and the following sums up what they may feel:

> When I ask you to listen to me and you start giving
> advice, you have not done what I asked.
> When I ask you to listen to me and you begin to tell
> me why I shouldn't feel that way, you are
> trampling on my feelings.
> When I ask you to listen to me and you feel you have
> to do something to solve my problem, you have
> failed me, strange as that may seem.
> Listen! All I asked was that you listen, not talk
> or do—just hear me [2, p. 127].

To listen with openness and caring is a skill. One that we can learn. Too often when we think we are listening we are actually waiting for a break in the conversation so we can respond. That is not listening. In the situation with our bereaved child, there are no words to take away the terrible finality of his or her loss.

To give the gift of listening requires commitment and patience. It takes true commitment to listen—with compassion, impartiality, and love—to our child talk about emotions and thoughts that are uncomfortable to us. It requires extreme patience to listen to our child's stories, feelings, and questioning over and over and over. If we feel the urge to hurry the story, interrupt, or mention the repetition, we are not listening.

Silence is another requirement for true, helpful listening. Resisting the urge to fill the silent moments in a conversation encourages closeness and sharing. Being attentive in posture also encourages closeness and indicates attentiveness. Leaning toward our child, holding eye contact, and hanging on his every word will indicate our listening and concern. Sitting close to our child whenever possible will encourage closeness and trust.

Our grieving child may require someone to listen at difficult and awkward times. If the conversation starts on a walk, in a shopping mall, restaurant, or even in a busy home, it may help to suggest moving to a quieter place to share time that is uninterrupted. If it is a phone conversation and there are distractions, we may move to a phone where we can give our full attention or explain the situation and call back as soon as possible and bring the conversation back to where it left off.

Questions can be important in listening if they are used infrequently and framed judiciously. Rather than parroting back what we think we heard our child say, we can try to sense what our child might be feeling and reflect that back.

Child: "I should have taken him to the doctor sooner."
Us: "It sounds like you are blaming yourself for Andy's death."

It may be necessary sometimes to ask for clarification and to encourage more talking. "Tell me about . . ." "What were you feeling when . . . ?" can be useful, but it is imperative that we check ourselves frequently for the amount of talking we are doing and make sure we are truly listening.

While listening, we will hear things we would rather not hear, have feelings that we would rather not feel, and even cry.

By being willing to tolerate those uncomfortable feelings and situations, we give our child and his or her spouse the priceless gift of truly being present.

Assuring our child that we will listen, no matter how terrible the thoughts or feelings might be, promotes a sense of trust and our child will feel better for having been able to talk about it. Through the listening and crying together a trusting relationship can develop that will serve both parties well throughout the rest of their lives.

REFERENCES

1. M. H. Gerner, *For Bereaved Grandparents,* The Centering Corporation, Omaha, Nebraska, 1990.
2. R. Houghton, Please Listen, as quoted in *The Promise of Green in the Season of Grief,* D. Roth (ed.), Riverrun Press, Piermont, New York, p. 127, 1987. The citation in this book is said to have been copied from *Trinity Reformed Chimes,* but I have seen the poem quoted with some of the words different, and attributed to Ray Roughton, in *Beyond Sympathy* by J. Harris, Pathfinder, Ventura, California, 1988, and many others places as "anonymous."

Chapter 7

SIBLING GRIEF AND NEEDS

We often refer to children as "forgotten mourners." Why?
Because they do grieve—the question is: do we create
conditions that allow them to mourn? Only when we as
caring adults encourage children to mourn, do we become
catalysts for healing [1, p. 39].

Alan Wolfelt

Grandparents can be one of the caring adults who encourage
surviving siblings to mourn. My son's family had two of them.
Stephanie, at six weeks of age, had different emotional
requirements than nine-year-old Curtis. Just as we adults
needed to develop new self-images based on a life without
Alex, so did Curtis. Developing a self-identity is a critical role
of the teenage years. Now in his mid-teens, Curtis says he just
started his grieving for Alex the last year or so. He claims he is
going over and remembering each day of Alex's illness, and
thinking about what it was like. The trauma of his own life-
threatening illness a year after Alex's death, and the subsequent and continuing treatment of that illness, certainly
contributed to Curtis' remembering very little of that period of
his life.

The reasons Curtis gives for his delayed response are, "It
just didn't sink in," and "I think I turned all my attention to
Stephanie." His assessment is, I believe, accurate and valid.
Embracing the full significance of Alex's death required major
adjustments for all the family. While shock and denial are just
as real to children as adults, their form may be different and

usually follows growth patterns. Children tend to mourn according to their developmental capacity.

Between the ages of eight and eleven, children's store of information expands, including their knowledge about disease, accidents, violence, and death. Thus they begin to conceptualize the causes of death much as adults do.

Curtis celebrated his ninth birthday just nine days before Alex died. At that age he was probably going through a transition that helped him recognize the permanence of death. Now in his teens, his expanded understanding of the depth of his loss and its finality helps him to realize "that death is personal" [2, p. 37].

Whatever Curtis now feels about the death of his baby brother, it is only part of his ongoing mourning process. My most vivid remembrance of Curtis at Alex's funeral was his look of stunned disbelief. Later he went off to play with friends, a behavior that is common for children his age.

We did, I believe, allow Curtis to mourn in his own way. Although he did not wish to go to the cemetery (and was not forced to go), he would readily discuss with us memories of Alex and asked questions about his death. For many of my visits to his home after Alex's death, Curtis and I would sit in Alex's room and talk about our memories and love for him.

Although Curtis never expressed any feelings of guilt, we realized the possibility of those thoughts being present. Children Curtis' age at the time of Alex's death may still have magical thinking—the belief that thoughts and words have more power than they do. We gave Curtis reassurances that thoughts and words do not kill, that they are not responsible for the death of a loved one.

Although taken in to see Alex after he died, Curtis, in retrospect, wishes he could have spent more time with him. How very difficult it is for parents and grandparents to know what is best for a child in such instances. We found that sometimes just being available to Curtis and Stephanie in such a period of intense grief required incredible effort.

David and Andrea worried about their ability to give Stephanie the time and attention they felt she needed as a small infant, and they worked hard to include Curtis in discussions to keep him abreast of what was happening. I believe that we all did our best to do what Jennifer Cadoff suggests, ". . . allow ourselves to be human" [3, p. 142].

At the very least we could attempt to be honest and let the children know that we hurt a great deal. Even if we can't find the right words, we can say that we aren't thinking as clearly as we would like because of our sadness. For the most part, we did not hide our emotions from Curtis and explained our distress to the best of our abilities.

John W. James, who founded the Grief Recovery Institute in Los Angeles following the death of his son in 1891, says, "The most helpful thing adults can do for children is to be emotionally honest about their own feelings" [3, p. 144]. I am convinced Curtis' parents did their very best to do just that. My efforts to be open and honest with him seemed so very difficult at times. Now I think of the situation as a classic case of "If I knew then, what I know now," for since then I have learned a great deal about how children grieve.

I did know intuitively, however, that some attitudes and comments were not useful. Suggesting to Curtis, for example, that "God took Alex because he loved him so much," is tantamount to suggesting 1) Curtis, or the rest of his family, didn't love Alex enough or he would still here, or 2) if God loved Curtis (parents, grandparents, Stephanie) enough God would take them also.

In my search for more information about how to relate better to my surviving grandson and granddaughter, I found some of the most useful information written by Alan D. Wolfelt. One of his major premises about grief is that we must allow children to teach us about their grief experiences and not to assume every child in a certain age group understands death the same way or has the same feelings. By remembering that healing through grief is a process not an event, and by listening to the children, we may learn what they require.

Some of the other admonitions Wolfelt has set forth are:

- Don't lie or tell half-truths to children.
- Don't wait for one big tell-all to begin to help children understand death.
- Encourage children to ask questions about death.
- Don't assume that children always grieve in some kind of orderly and predictable way.
- Let children know that you really want to understand.
- Don't misunderstand children's grief process that may seem, to adults, like a lack of feelings.
- Allow children to participate in the funeral.
- Don't forget about the concept of magical thinking; that thoughts and words have the power to create illness, injury, and death.
- Remember that feeling relief doesn't mean a lack of love.
- Realize that children's bodies react when they experience grief.
- Don't feel bad when you don't have all the answers for your grandchild about religion or death.
- Keep in mind that grief is complicated [4, p. 28].

One of the most useful articles I read in my studies about children's grief came from the 1992 January and February issues of *Bereavement* magazine. In those two issues Wolfelt wrote about the "Ten Common Myths About Children and Grief" [5, pp. 38-39]. Some of those myths, those erroneous ideas, were particularly applicable to our family's experience:

A child's grief and mourning is of short duration.

Mourning is a process. What seems like a lack of feeling by children is a child's way of protecting themselves from the hurt of the loss. Something as simple as running out to play with their friends helps them normalize their situation and thus helps them cope with the death of a loved one.

There is a predictable and orderly stage-like progression to the experiences of grief and mourning.

The stages of grief popularized by Elisabeth Kübler-Ross [6] helped people understand grief and mourning better, but are only guidelines for what is a disorderly and unpredictable experience.

Infants and toddlers are too young to grieve and mourn.

There isn't any sure way of knowing how Stephanie felt at the time of Alex's death. She surely had to have been affected by the pain and anguish around her. What we do know, however, is that as her cognitive skills have increased she has mourned Alex, the loss of a brother she knows only through pictures and our reminisces.

Children are not affected by the grief and mourning of the adults who surround them.

How we mourn is usually a reflection of what we learned in our own families. We learn from the modeling of our parents. Hiding our grief will teach our children to hide their feelings. By allowing ourselves to mourn, we may teach our children the capacity to love and consequently the need to mourn.

The goal in helping bereaved children is to "get them over" grief and mourning.

Bereaved children, like bereaved adults, may become reconciled to their grief, but any attempt to resolve bereaved children's grief, especially in any preconceived manner or time, is actually destructive to the healing process.

My eight-week training at New Song (Center for Grieving Children and Those Who Love Them)[1] gave me new insights

---

[1] New Song, 6947 E McDonald Dr., Paradise Valley, AZ 85253, (602) 951-8985.

into children's grief. One of the most important attitudes held by the loving people at New Song is Dr. Alan Wolfelt's assertion that the medical model of assessment, diagnosis, and treatment does not work with grief, but rather the work of mourning is to reach a reconciliation or accommodation. Grief is never resolved, mourning never ends, it just has less-frequent outward manifestations.

Another author, Don Schaefer, advises not to judge children's mourning or try to stop the process, as that minimizes the loss and puts an unbelievable burden on the child. Through nonjudgmental listening, we can assist surviving siblings because, "Once a feeling is expressed, no matter how negative, it doesn't have the power that it did when it was formless. When feelings are put on the table, talked out and looked at in a realistic perspective, they often lose their impact" [7, p. 85].

Children mourn through behavior, and we may help them best by learning and understanding their needs behind that behavior. What must be taken into account when attempting to help a child is that each child's response to death is influenced by many factors:

- The relationship with the person who died. (The more complicated the relationship, the more complicated the mourning.)
- The nature of the death. (Anticipated or sudden and the specific cause, whether a long illness or traumatic.)
- Support system. (Which includes the intra-psychic health of the individual and the attitudes, beliefs, behaviors, and responsiveness of the child's family.)
- Chronological/developmental age. (Ability to understand and process loss is different for each age.)
- Personality. (A child's unique personality will give a distinct expression to his or her grief.)
- Prior experience with death. (A previous loss will impact on the current loss. Attitudes and behaviors learned from previous losses will also surface with new losses.)

- Ritual/funeral experience. (An opportunity to face the reality of death in a supportive atmosphere will help a child mourn.)
- Cultural background. (The beliefs and values of a child's cultural background will help shape a child's mourning.)

I think Curtis displayed an underlying fear of losing another sibling by his great concern for Stephanie's well-being. He frequently scolded me for not "watching her close enough," when she would fall or tumble from something. Stephanie learned to walk while Curtis was hospitalized, so I sat at one end of the yard and tape-recorded her efforts. Upon seeing the video, Curtis became upset about her toddling around the pool while I sat "so far away."

Curtis could verbally express many of his emotions and distract himself with friends, books, and TV. Stephanie, however, required more frequent attention. We endeavored to give her all the love, holding, and cuddling she required. So diligent were we that when it came time for her to learn to crawl, and then walk, we had to remind each other that she needed to be put down where she could do just that.

Cognizant of the ongoing process of mourning, I wrote a letter to Stephanie (eventually 5 pages, single-spaced) that I finished in the summer of 1992. In the letter I told Stephanie how wonderful she is and how I experienced her birth and subsequent experiences with her and her family. It is something that she can keep and read whenever she feels the desire. Stephanie's letter is only one example of the attempts I have made to help my surviving grandchildren.

Maintaining close relationships with surviving siblings can be one way grandparents can offer special support. Helping my grandchildren in as many ways as possible also helps a little to reduce the agony of watching my son and daughter-in-law grieve. Those children are best served, I believe, when we set our priorities to recognize their immediate and ongoing needs. We all have limited resources of emotional and physical strength as well as, for most of us, financial ones. These resources require careful rationing as we attempt to reconcile our loss while assisting our grieving grandchild(ren) and his or her family in the grieving process.

Many of our modern technologies allow relatively quick and easy access to family members, even over long distances. The telephone is one such familiar convenience that can given us quick, accessible means (to the limit of our financial ability) of connection with our grandchildren. That technology gave us comfort during Alex's hospitalization, as we could pick up the phone, even in his ICU room, and make contact with family members in other cities and states. Even small babies enjoy hearing a grandparent's voice and will come to recognize it. Since none of our children live in the same city as we do, and since two of our children (including David and Andrea's family) live in another state, the telephone has remained an important method of contact.

There are numerous methods of keeping in contact with and helping grieving grandchildren. Most of the organizations (and many other local, state, and national ones) that are listed in the Bibliography have special books for grieving children. Compassionate Friends also has a newsletter for surviving siblings. Articles in newspapers and magazines, newsletters, and books often discuss the special role that grandparents play in their grandchildren's lives. Some of the many suggestions for sustaining a loving bond with grandchildren include:

- Exchanging audio and/or video tapes.
  A cassette tape or video of a grandparent reading a favorite story or telling stories about the family, the pet, special projects or, with a video, showing new and different places, demonstrating how to do something can all be a connecting force.
- Communicate by mail.
  Yes, the mail can still be a good method of contacting your grandchildren. All grandchildren, including the very young, enjoy mail that is addressed to them, even before they are capable of reading it. For those who like to write, a letter can be of enormous comfort and help to those who receive it. One of the really nice aspects of

letters, I believe, is that they allow us to receive the communication on our time. For children, a letter, postcard, or photo gives them something tangible to hold onto from distant grandparents.

For those grandparents who have frequent and close contact with their grandchildren, ideas for tightening that bond include:

• Taking a grandchild on a trip to the library, lunch, or a stroll in the park offers opportunities to develop lasting relationships with grandchildren.
• Inviting a grandchild to go on trips, camping, backpacking, rafting, fishing, sightseeing. Our oldest granddaughter has traveled with us many times.
• Joining a grandchild in a favorite activity when possible. One of my fondest memories with a grandchild is going roller skating with my eldest granddaughter even though I had not skated for many (40 maybe) years.
• Teaching a new skill to a grandchild. Another of my fond memories will always be of starting four of my grandchildren on ice skates, and it had also been a long time since I had been on ice.
• Asking a grandchild to teach you something. All I know about board games I have learned from my grandchildren. Our grandchildren are often much more adept and proficient at some of the technologies of our age than we are and are usually more than happy to show us how to use them.

It is not of the foremost importance that I always say the right words, or do the right thing, but rather let my grandchildren know I love them and that they are special. Although Alex's surviving siblings live in another state, I make numerous trips to visit with them, call them frequently, and send letters and packages. There are numerous books available on how to help children mourn, but I suspect just being available and keeping in touch is one of the best gifts a grandparent can give.

REFERENCES

1. A. Wolfelt, Ten Common Myths About Children and Grief, *Bereavement Magazine,* January 1992.
2. D. Seibert, J. C. Drolet, and J. V. Fetro, *Are You Sad Too?* ETR Associates, Santa Cruz, California, 1993.
3. J. Cadoff, How Kids Grieve, *Parents,* April 1993.
4. A. Wolfelt, *A Child's View of Grief,* Service Corporation International, Denver, 1990.
5. A. Wolfelt, Ten Common Myths About Children and Grief, Part I & Part II, *Bereavement Magazine,* pp. 38-39, January/February 1992.
6. E. Kübler-Ross, *On Death and Dying,* Macmillan, New York, 1969.
7. D. Schaefer and C. Lyons, *How Do We Tell the Children,* Newmarket Press, New York, 1986.

Chapter 8

IN MEMORY: MEMORIALS AND HEALING RITUALS

In the rising of the sun
and in its going down:
we remember them.
In the blowing of the wind
and in the chill of winter:
we remember them . . .
So long as we live
They too shall live
For they are now a part of us:
As we remember them [1].

My husband and I sent the preceding poem in our 1989 Christmas cards as a way of honoring the memory of Alex. We felt the poem eloquently expressed our belief that "Every death leaves its scars on the griever and part of a healthy recovery is in remembering" [2, p. 51].

Cultures dictate formal ceremonies memorializing the death of a loved one. Those traditional observances serve to ". . . lend a sense of importance to our rite of passage; put our beliefs into action; give form to human life; bring support from the community whether it is one or more people; and offer permission to grieve" [3, p. 143]. The intent of those formal rituals is to offer spiritual strength and direction. Rites of passage, particularly for a child's death, are often over just as our grief begins. Additional personal ceremonies are beneficial

73

during the prolonged period of grief following prescribed death
rites.

BURIAL

Making arrangements for the burial of a small child must
rank as one of the most excruciating experiences anyone can
experience. Even as I write this many years later, the whole
concept feels overwhelming and repugnant. Andrea's father
took care of most of the formal arrangements with the mor-
tuary. My recollection is of how I worried about how to support, without intruding on, David and Andrea's decisions
regarding the ceremony. I felt tremendous pain and compassion for both David and Andrea as I watched them work
through that process. They did ask me for help when planning
the music for the funeral, specifically for identifying Mozart's
Eine kleine Nachtmusik that Alex had enjoyed since infancy.
Their asking for that assistance helped me to feel useful at a
time I was attempting to be available for whatever they might
ask.

David and Andrea followed an ancient burial practice of
placing items of personal importance to them and their family
in Alex's casket. They also put in "Ernie," a stuffed animal I
had bought and mailed to him early in his illness. To this day
I do not remember what I planned to do, or where I planned to
go, when I drove by a toy store and suddenly decided I needed
to stop, buy, and mail something to my sick little grandson.
How very glad I am that I did just that. "Ernie," a small
stuffed toy, became a favorite of Alex's during his illness and
we had stuck it between the slats of his crib at the hospital. In
the middle of that first long, sleepless night, Alex called out
"Ernie," as he wanted to hold the toy. It was to be one of the
few clear words I heard Alex speak while hospitalized despite
the fact he had been talking in complete sentences before
falling ill.

Alex is buried in a cemetery only minutes away from his
parents' home. Since cemeteries are a place where people may
be themselves and weeping is allowed, most of our family has

done that often. Attending to Alex's grave is a ritual of remembrance and love. Like that long line of grieving human beings before us, our family places flowers, toys, balloons, and other special items at Alex's grave-site, especially on his birthday, death date, and other significant holidays. His grave is marked with a headstone proclaiming, "Too Precious To Keep." My own "precious" son cleans up and trims the grass around the headstone, sets up a Christmas tree and star which the family gathers at dusk on Christmas Eve to light.

Through the Christmas ritual, as well as others throughout the year, we shift "our focus from our daily lives through ritual" [3, p. 143]. These acts allow us a special place and time to remember—a time to acknowledge our love and loss of Alex, that then allows us to turn to the present and the enjoyment of current blessings.

Special gifts to each other accompanied the Christmas Eve lighting ceremony for the first few years. Andrea gave members of the immediate family International Star Registry certificates one year. The certificates signified the re-designation of a numbered star to the name of Alexander. The official registry is printed only every other year, so David gave the book as a special gift the next year.

DONATIONS

One donation, in memory of Alex, I gave to the local hospice as a Christmas memorial. A white card in the shape of a dove held his name, birth, and death dates. The card hung with hundreds of others from a sixty-foot-high Christmas tree erected in a local urban park. When I first beheld the tree, I despaired of ever finding Alex's particular card, but as if directed I found it almost immediately. I took a photograph of the tree and its lovely surroundings and gave it to David and Andrea.

Other seasonal observances have included donations of lilies at Easter and poinsettias at Christmas to my church in memory of Alex. If not picked up after the service by those who donate them, the flowers are delivered to shut-ins and nursing homes—a fitting place, I believe, for them to go.

These seasonal observances satisfy a need for our family, and they fulfill the qualifications defined by Beck and Metrick: "To derive the power from a ritual it must, in some way, stand apart from our ordinary lives" [4, p. 7].

MUSIC

There are countless modes of achieving benefits from private ritual. Listening to music is one of my favorites. While I enjoy all types, it is to classical music, and particularly the music of Jean Sibelius and Edvard Grieg, to which I turn for refuge and comfort. Perhaps their music speaks to me of my Northern European ancestry. By placing myself in the center of the stereo speakers, I can feel the music as well as hear it and give myself completely to the sensations of being suffused and transported by the sounds.

Music has great associative powers. Soon after Alex's death, my son compiled an audio tape of music specific to his memory of Alex. Although special for David, the tape touched all of those who heard it, and became a favorite tape for my other grandchildren. When I subsequently developed a video in memory of Alex, I used music from that tape as background music.

VIDEO

We have no actual video of Alex. Although none of us owned a camcorder, we often discussed renting one. We never did. We did take countless pictures and slides of Alex, however, and I put them on video with the aforementioned music and a narration of his life. I gave the video to his parents as a gift the second Christmas after his death.

The background music for the video included Mozart's *Eine kleine Nachtmusik*. We had started Alex listening to classical music soon after his birth and the Mozart music was one of his favorites.

LETTERS

When I arrived home following Alex's death, one of my first acts was to write commendation letters for those Intensive Care nurses who had worked so competently and diligently in attending Alex. The letters were something David and Andrea wanted written but felt incapable of doing at the time. Writing the letters gave me an opportunity to remember Alex and a method of expressing my family's appreciation of the respect and love he had received from the medical staff.

I also wrote long letters to the two Intensive Care doctors who supervised Alex's treatments and to several other specialists called in for consultation. Most of the time during Alex's hospitalization, one or the other of the two primary care physicians was present in the Intensive Care Unit, and we never doubted their dedication to their young patients.

The major portions of the letters were of appreciation for their expert care and understanding. However, I also included some comments regarding the handling of communications. I objected strongly to the method of transmission used in conveying information from physician to family. The habit, particularly by one of the doctors, of discussing Alex's condition in front of him always distressed me. Children, I believe, may not understand the words, but they certainly sense the atmosphere of fear and confusion.

Questions always arise in survivors' minds about what could or should have been done differently. I believe I conveyed to the physicians, without undo animosity, my concerns and questions about their methods of communicating with parents and family, thus reducing some of the power of that memory.

Through those letters I tried to memorialize my beloved grandson, while giving sincere recognition of appreciation. It is my hope that in some small way my observations will lead to the easing of fear and confusion for some other young patient. Information is power, I believe. Conveying to the medical staff our feelings about the care and respect given

Alex, I believe, will benefit other children. Through that act I hoped to perpetuate some of the best of Alex.

PERSONAL RITUALS

Since I live in another state, the conventional "grave visit" is infrequent. Fortunately I live where we have flowers, especially roses, blooming almost year round. Cutting a flower and placing it in a special vase on my kitchen counter is a routine that has become an almost daily ritual for me. It is an act that typifies what Sam Keen means when he says, "Ritual invests ordinary acts and objects with 'symbolic' meaning" [5, p. 262].

There are many ways of investing ordinary acts and objects with symbolic meaning. Planting trees as a memorial to a loved one has become fairly common in our society. Several years after Alex's death, his parents had a magnolia tree planted in a "green belt" close to where they live and where they may view it every day when they drive by. They asked me to write a dedication for the tree:

Magnolia Tree Dedication

Because we, his family, will carry forever the loving memory of Alex in our hearts, we are here today to honor that memory with the dedication of this magnolia tree.

Magnolias are an ancient and noble tree. Geologists tell us that magnolias have been on the earth for as much as eight to 100 million years. The ancestors of our present-day species of trees were growing in the forests while the great dinosaurs still roamed the earth. The genus magnolia was named by Linnaeus in honor of Pierre Magnol, physician to King Louis XIV of France, and director of a botanical garden at Montpellier.

Growing to heights of 60 to 80 feet, the leathery leaves, creamy-white flowers and egg-shaped fruit are the magnolia's outstanding characteristics. This magnolia tree, planted here in memory of Alex, was chosen not only for its outstanding characteristics, but specifically because the extremely large, wonderfully beautiful flowers open in June.

With a star in the constellation, Capricornus, named
after him, it seems only fitting that heaven and earth are
joined in Alex's memory through that star and this magnificent tree.

At Christmas the family puts a big red bow on the tree,
and, appropriately, the first year after planting the tree bore a
single white blossom in June.

WRITING

One of the most useful activities for myself and Alex's
mother has been writing. Journals are an oft-recommended
action for many situations. Both Andrea and I have found
writing useful for processing our grief. Giving voice to our
agony through the written word has helped to defuse some of
the pain.

Obviously my writing this book is an act of remembrance,
as is the dedication poem I wrote almost in its entirety the
night after my father-in-law's memorial service. He died four
years after Alex, and his memorial service brought back
memories of Alex. The poem was most insistent on being
written. We were in a motel room in another state when the
poem first formed in my mind. I arose, took paper and pen into
the bathroom to write so as not to disturb my sleeping husband. Twice I did that same activity, to finish and refine the
poem, until it finally allowed me to rest for the night. Ultimately I had the poem published with a photo as a memorial
to Alex in the June 1993 *Bereavement Magazine.*

PRIVATE MEMORIALS

Remembering our loved one is a means of transmuting
grief to creativity. Those methods can be as varied as there are
people who grieve. Other grandparents have told me about, or
I have read about, various other types of memorials which
include:

- Writing letters to the deceased. (Often the letters are burned at a private ceremony, thus symbolically releasing the survivor of possible worries, fears, and anger.)
- Releasing helium balloons with the name of the deceased attached, or notes.
- Planting of a tree, placement of special benches or plaques in public parks.
- Painting a memorial work.
- Working in clay to develop memorial items.
- Small memorials or shrines in the home.

Grief counselors feel that keeping a child's room as it was before death for a long length of time may lead to complications of grieving. A small area dedicated to remembrance of a child, including pictures, however, is appropriate.

Although difficult at first, both David and Andrea's home, and ours, continue to prominently display our favorite pictures of Alex. His room remained much the same for a number of months and often became a haven for us when we needed to actively mourn. Curtis would take me into Alex's room when I visited, and we would talk about him. Curtis would also ask my advice about which of Alex's toys I thought might be appropriate (and which his parents would approve) to give to Stephanie. It became a very touching ritual he and I went through on many of my visits.

MEMORIES

Memory as a memorial to a loved one is a natural process. Often my remembering comes in unexpected moments of my life—those singular instants that draw my attention, connecting me with life and the world around me—a bird song, a musical melody, a magnificent view, a lovely flower, a comely child. They are often recollection that are unforeseeable, that seize me unaware and flood me with painful memories. Sometimes the trigger is clear, as when a child looks like Alex, or something that reminds me of how my son enjoyed life before Alex died.

Other times, I can't explain what it is about the way a bird flies or a particular piece of music, but it crushes my chest and leaves me gasping. I feel exposed, not knowing how to protect myself "from these unbidden memories" as discussed by Barbara D. Rosof in her book, *The Worst Loss* [6, p. 83].

Memory triggers are just as idiosyncratic as any other behavior, and that natural force of recall is a personal dynamic. I can remember through an act of consciousness or as part of a ritual. More often than not, however, my reminiscences are pauses that come unbidden, as they do to the character in *Missing Joseph*.

> Funny, how he could still miss Annie at an unexpected moment like this. It always came without warning—a quick surge of grief and longing that rose from his loins and ended near his heart—and it always came from something so ordinary that he never considered how insidious was the action that precipitated it. He was always unarmed and never unaffected [7, p. 137].

None of us is ever "unaffected." Memory is such a tricky and sometimes cruel gift and not always in our control. Sometimes it fails us, other times it surprises and assaults us. I suspect that I will have moments of remembering that generate longing and painful feelings for the rest of my life.

We had Alex for what seemed a very short time. One of my friends on seeing a photograph I had taken of Alex at six months of age said, "That's an old soul." Perhaps, for those who believe in karma and reincarnation, Alex only needed to spend that short a time here. We, his family, however, will always feel we needed him for a much longer time. But we will continue to work at being one of those families that have integrated their sorrow and loss into their lives through recalling vivid memories, thus keeping a connection with their deceased loved one.

REFERENCES

1. Jewish Prayer for Children, *Gates of Prayer,* Reform Judaism Prayer Book.
2. B. Kreis and A. Pattie, *Up From Grief,* Seabury Press, New York, 1969.
3. C. M. Sanders, *How to Survive the Loss of a Child,* Prima, Rocklin, California, 1992.
4. R. Beck and S. B. Metrick, *The Art of Ritual,* Celestial Arts, Berkeley, California, 1990.
5. S. Keen, *Hymns to an Unknown God,* Bantam Books, New York, 1994.
6. B. D. Rosof, *The Worst Loss,* Henry Holt and Company, New York, 1994.
7. E. George, *Missing Joseph,* Bantam Books, New York, 1993.

Chapter 9

HOW OTHERS MAY HELP/HINDER

The best thing that friends and relatives can do is to accompany grieving parents (grandparents) in their sadness [1, p. 15].

Laura Grimes

A difficult task—to accompany someone in their sadness. So troublesome and uncomfortable is the journey that many tend to minimize, or attempt to diminish, grieving. "While (such) efforts to reduce someone's grieving may seem," as Ira Nerken says, "justified as acts of love, and motivated only by a wish to minimize another's pain, and thus are difficult, especially for the bereaved, to challenge, they fail the first test of love: they do not show respect" [2, p. 1091].

Our family received acts of love even before Alex died. On the day of his death my cousin and his wife drove a great distance to be with us at the hospital. They stayed with and cared for baby Stephanie so we could give our undivided attention to Alex and each other. One of Andrea's nursing friends also made the long trip that day to give us her support.

The most respect shown me came from those who recognized and comprehended grief's impact on my life. Some of my close friends sent flowers to Alex's funeral, and a number of my family, friends, and acquaintances sent cards. Neighbors visited soon after my return home, as did official emissaries of my church. All were demonstrating their regard for my sorrow. Although obviously difficult for some, I appreciated those who made the effort to visit me in my home. I needed their presence, and a hug really helped. Being there acknowledged my loss, and tolerating my crying was an added bonus. How well the novelist Elizabeth George understood the needs of the sorrowing.

> He had drawn her into his arms with five simple words which effectively freed her to be who and what she really was for the rest of her life: "It's all right to cry" [3, p. 362].

And cry I did, often alone. I felt those around me would not, could not, understand the depth of my sorrow. My feelings of pain and helplessness warped my sense of time so that the support I did receive was quickly forgotten. Suffering the raw emotion of loss left me susceptible to the disappointed expectation I had of those I wanted to hear from, either by a phone call, letter, or visit. One example included the neglect I felt by many of those I had known and sang with in choir, in some cases almost a quarter of a century. The official visits from the church I welcomed. I craved the comfort of well-known people.

Gradually I became aware of my need to be authentic, to be true to my feelings, no matter how frightful they might be. Those who made themselves available, who tolerated and accepted my changed, often gloomy self, were of immense help to me. It was not easy to befriend me.

In the past I have found it difficult to give comfort and convey words of consolation. I am not alone. Deborah Roth, in her book *Stepping Stones to Grief Recovery,* mentions a collection of condolence letters by famous poets and writers, and how stilted and self-conscious-sounding their words of condolence. She wrote, "the most effective letter of the lot was written by George Bernard Shaw to a loved one whose son had been killed in the war. It says simply, 'I heard the news. Damn, damn, damn, damn!' " [4, p. 111]. That expression works for me!

WHAT HELPED

Early in our bereavement, some of the most useful comments made to me and my family (and to others with whom I have spoken) included:

- What a terrible tragedy.
- I can't imagine how you feel.
- Some things make no sense.
- How horrible (difficult) this must be for you.
- Do you want to talk about it?
- You must feel like the pain will never end.
- Crying is O.K.
- "What a bummer" and "pooh," while sounding irreverent nevertheless indicated a sense of speechlessness many felt, and therefore conveyed a real degree of empathy.

Comments that validated my feelings were a Godsend to my raw emotions of new grief. Even more useful would have been statements that denoted a more active caring that not only would have been supportive mentally and emotionally, but also physically.

- I will call soon. (And *do* it!)
- Let's go to lunch. (Now, today!)
- I will bring you dinner today.
- Let me go to the store for you.

Not very many of my friends knew Alex, but those who were willing to talk about him gave me wonderful support. Over and over I have heard from parents and grandparents how important it is to talk about their child, to have others share stories about them. One of my friends who had lost a teenage son told me the story of a neighbor sharing her recollection of an over-the-fence conversation she had had with her son. The topic, my friend said, "was insignificant and of no importance, but she gave me back a part of him I would otherwise never have had and it made me happy."[1]

Sympathy cards do help. And cards remembering special occasions such as birthday and death dates are truly cherished. I found someone just calling to say "hello" and chat

---

[1] Personal correspondence.

gave me a welcome respite from my ennui and sadness. Every effort to help was cherished. My family and I recognized the effort each made, whether it was a phone call, visit, or more active help. Unfortunately, as most others in our situations, we probably did a poor job of letting those who helped know how much they were appreciated.

Needing someone to listen to my obsessive desire to talk about Alex (a perfectly normal reaction to grief), more often than not, demanded too much from friends and family. In grief groups I found that essential patience and support. Grief groups vary to a great extent, and may not be for everyone. It is critical, however, to find a method of sharing the ongoing grief because, even if someone has shared our loss, their feelings of grief will be different than ours. The empathy and acceptance from others, however, can make it easier to go on, for "A large part of moving on involves taking the experience within you and putting it outside where the burden is not just yours to carry" [5, p. 28].

Sharing in grief groups helped me move on. An added benefit of grief groups, I found, included learning new methods of understanding and support that then assisted me in being available and helpful to my bereaved children and grandchildren.

As a grandparent I feel I have more life knowledge, more communicative skills, and possibly more tolerance than my children. I am in a unique position to impart information about my family's needs. If I keep my communication honest and kind, perhaps I may teach others some of the things we have learned about grief.

The useful ideas I have gleaned from my experience and studies over these past years are applicable to both grandparents and parents. Besides my knowledge from conversations and correspondence with other grandparents and working in grief groups, more specific and organized information has come from the many grief books I have read, from seminars on grief, from "The Compassionate Friends Newsletters," and from *Bereavement Magazine*. These sources, combined with my own observations and feelings, are compiled in the following list of what I consider to be the most beneficial and appreciated.

THINGS TO REMEMBER

- Please don't avoid me, but have the courage to accept me and my grief.
- Please be aware that each death is unique and cannot be compared. Grief is not a competitive sport.
- Asking "how are you feeling" indicates a recognition of my feelings and a willingness to listen, and is preferable to "how are you?"
- When with me, please try not to be embarrassed or, worse yet, try to stop me if I start to cry when I suddenly see, hear, or smell something that reminds me of Alex.

These are difficult requests, and ask a great deal of those who would journey with the grieving. If understood, however, such efforts will be of great assistance, as will talking about the deceased.

- Please speak the name of my grandchild, for that child lived and remains important to me.
- Understand that crying and becoming emotional when talking about my grandchild (or my son and his family) is because my grandchild died, not because of your mentioning him or his family. Allowing me to cry is healing.
- If you have special memories of Alex, please share them with me.
- If you have pictures or other remembrances in your home of my grandchild, please do not remove them.

All the best efforts of those that would accompany another in their sadness, however, will not completely alleviate the sorrow or the results of that pain.

- Try to understand some days are good, and some not so good. Please don't suggest on good days that my grief is over, or on bad days that I need professional help.

- Accept me as I am. Weight loss or gain, fatigue, illnesses, and being accident prone are only a few manifestations of the body's typical reactions to grief.
- Tolerate my "crazies" that include anger, frustration, helplessness, and depression for they are common reactions to the loss of a grandchild.
- My grandchild's birthday, death date, and other holidays (mother's and father's day, etc.), are very difficult times for me and my family, and we would appreciate knowing you are thinking of us on those occasions.

Because most of us want to help when we see someone in pain, we tend to want to give advice as a means of assistance. Usually, such advice is ill conceived and unwanted, especially that which goes against the needs of the sorrowing.

- Please don't suggest I take drugs, drink, or attempt to coerce me into cheerfulness to alleviate my pain; the pain of grief must be experienced to facilitate healing.
- Please don't tell me I shouldn't reexamine my faith, values, and beliefs; those things will be questioned after the death of a child, and an understanding listener while I struggle would be appreciated.
- Please don't expect my grief to be over in a few months; the first few years will be especially difficult.

And, finally, remember that waiting for me to get back to my old self will be a long wait—grief changes people. I will never be the same person I was before my grandchild died.

Many people must have recognized my state of shock that continued even after I returned to my own home. In retrospect I am surprised no one (other than my husband) offered any physical or practical help. I was gone from my home almost a month. Two-and-a-half weeks of that time was spent at the hospital with the horror and agony of Alex's death. Then came his funeral, and all the while I tried to care for my children and grandchildren. I was mentally, emotionally, and physically exhausted.

My husband had spent time with me there also, so our house was dirty, the yard needed mowing and serious watering, lots of dirty laundry needed to be done, and we had few groceries. I was too weary and depressed to do anything about any of it, much less cook a proper meal. I could have used some actual physical help in doing much needed domestic chores.

WHAT HINDERS

The least anyone can do for someone who is grieving is not to hinder. Perhaps the worst hindrance (causing distress) is avoidance. David and Andrea will always remember the people who dodged them in the grocery store. It is one thing to not call or visit, but actual shunning adds to the devastating feelings following the death of a beloved child.

There are people in my life that have never mentioned Alex's death. For those with whom I had contact, the one viewpoint I found most difficult, and still do, is when someone believes my tears are pathetic signs of weakness or helplessness, and my distress and confusion are abnormalities. Those people are not only disrespectful, but hinder my grief process.

"Throughout our lives most of us spend some time being comforted, being the comforter, being consoled or being the consoler," writes Erin Linn in *I Know Just How You Feel: Avoiding the Clichés of Grief.* Linn says it is important to ". . . find new ways to approach the bereaved through love that is sensitive and productive" [6, pp. ix-x]. She also believes that, "what may appear as insensitive comments from relatives and friends are really words of love" [6, p. x]. Genuine desire to express love and care will be recognized, I believe, but there are any number of attitudes and comments that are undeniably *not* helpful, such as:

The most totally useless comment:

- Call me if there is anything I can do. (The bereaved are overwhelmed with their pain, unable, in most cases, to even think of what they need, much less generate the energy to call and ask someone for help.)

The most frequent injunctions:

- Cheer up.
- Count your blessings.
- Don't cry.
- Don't think about it, think about something else.
- Let's change the subject.
- Time will heal.
- Think about your other children (grandchildren).
- Go out more, get a hobby, puppy, etc.

As annoying and downright stressful at times as injunctions were and are, I feel they usually convey an honest attempt at assistance. Some other comments, however, I can only call:

Platitudes, patronizing, and sometimes simply dumb comments:

- I know how you feel.
- It makes me depressed to hear you talk about it.
- Oh, if it happened to me, I'd die.
- You will have other children (grandchildren).
- You do have other children (grandchildren) don't you?
- He won't suffer from pain, illnesses, etc.
- Have you tried doing your grieving differently, various exercises, etc.

Absolutely the most disrespectful of all comments are those that Erin Linn calls "God cliches" [6, p. 76]:

- He is better off now, he is in heaven.
- It was meant to be, it was God's will.
- Where is your faith?
- If you just had more faith!
- God never gives us more than we can handle.

Laura Grimes, in "What not to Say to a Grieving Parent," addresses several of the above with the response,

> No matter how strong one's faith, the loss of a loved one is a source of great sadness and often anger at God. This is all the more true when a child has died, when life has scarcely begun and so many unrealized possibilities remain . . . To dwell on the child's presumed happiness in heaven suggests that there is something good about the death" [1, pp. 15-18].

There was nothing good about Alex's death. Those who tried, and still try, to convince or comfort me with that type of rationalization show enormous disrespect for my pain and suffering. One such individual, on being asked to review an early draft of this manuscript, responded with a long note about how a child is "without sin, and therefore, guaranteed a special in heaven." Somehow she thought this would ease my pain. She ended the note with the trite argument, " 'Suffer the little children to come to me,' if we can accept this biblical quotation, we can find solace in a grandchild's passing." Even the term *passing* indicates her avoidance of the reality of the death. She falls in that group of people "who think they know." These are not supportive, useful people. As one friend said, "those kinds of people you do not need to keep in your life."

My pain and sorrow were precipitated by my loss, and no amount of rationalization will change that. Much of the discomfort of being around the bereaved, says Deborah Roth, ". . . is our fear of death. We don't like to be reminded of our vulnerability" [4, p. 112]. It takes a great deal of courage to find a way around or through that discomfort of being close to the bereaved. A true awareness of someone's grief begins only if we have suffered similar losses. Even then, we cannot know exactly how someone else feels, how profound that particular loss is for them. I believe it is of utmost importance to accept this limitation and simply be available to listen, and not offer advice. In such a manner does someone pass the "first test of love," by showing respect.

REFERENCES

1. L. M. Grimes, What Not to Say to a Grieving Parent, *U.S. Catholic,* April 1993.
2. I. Nerken, Making It Safe to Grieve, *The Christian Century,* November 30, 1988.
3. E. George, *A Suitable Vengeance,* Bantam Books, New York, 1991.
4. D. Roth (ed.), *Stepping Stones to Grief Recovery,* IBS Press, Santa Monica, California, 1987.
5. S. B. Metrick, *Crossing the Bridge: Creating Ceremonies for Grieving and Healing From Life's Losses,* Celestial Arts, Berkeley, California, 1994.
6. E. Linn, *I Know Just How You Feel: Avoiding the Clichés of Grief,* The Publisher's Mark, Incline Village, Nevada, 1986.

Chapter 10

FINDING MY WAY

One way to learn courage is to experiment with being courageous . . . We can taste courage, notice courage, pretend courage, and most of all we can try it out for ourselves. Having the courage to grieve leads to having the courage to live, to love, to risk . . . [1, p. 10].

Judy Tatelbaum

The loss of Alex irrevocably changed my life. To assimilate the reality of his death and subsequently convert my relationship with him into a memory that no longer preoccupied would require great courage. I doubted my ability to do the subtle and complex negotiations required for such a forbidding task.

With the death of his cherished son, I realized that my son would be forever changed also. This awareness added not only more sorrow but complexity to my burden. Gone was the happy confident young man I had known as my son. I had always considered David to be my most passionate and sentimental child and had recognized his profound love for Alex.

Now, David often appeared to me to have become old, haggard, and defeated. I could not take away his pain; could not return to him his beloved child. What could I possibly do to help him? And how, and in what way, could I support myself from this double infliction of sadness?

At some level I knew that time, patience, and the courage to make difficult choices would be needed. For a long time after Alex's death all of this seemed beyond me. A moment of clear thought and intent would disappear rapidly into the chasm of my sorrow.

What I had wanted was for Alex to have survived his illness. In my dreams I saw him. Alive. Sometimes during waking moments my mind would momentarily refuse to acknowledge the terrible fact that he was dead. I would make plans for him and his family. Then would follow the waking, or recalling, and the searing pain would come again.

My attachment to Alex had been a powerful, special bond. As a grandparent, I did not need to concern myself with Alex's daily care. At the time of his birth, I had more maturity, affluence, and especially time than I had had almost a decade earlier when Curtis and their older cousin, Starr, were born. I also had an increased level of patience and tolerance. Without parental worries and fears, I was free to join Alex and Curtis in their explorations and games. They had acted as a prism through which I could see the world in ways that were inaccessible to me through my own children. Seeing the world through the wonder of my grandchildren's eyes renewed my faith in humanity and my hope for the future. And then that future shattered.

For Alex's funeral, his parents felt that white limousines for the hearse and family transportation would be appropriate, and Andrea and I also wore white. That sense of purity of heart helped us to think of him as being an angel. David and Andrea's home now holds a collection of angel artifacts. We have all purchased at one time or another, and especially at Christmas time, something in the shape of an angel or with an angel image.

Andrea, Curtis, and Stephanie had an experience they believe involved angelic protection from Alex. They had gone shopping some distance from home. When they prepared to leave the store, Andrea discovered that one of the expensive shoes I had bought Stephanie was missing. After searching the store and not being able to find it, Andrea had finally left a message with the manager to please call if they found the shoe. Then, as the three of them drove home on the freeway they came upon a terrible car accident. Andrea felt sure that they would have been involved if they had left the store when planned. Her confidence in an angelic intervention increased when a store employee called the next morning to say they had found the shoe.

Although our current pet, Kitty Cat, may not qualify as an angelic protector, she brought us great comfort at a difficult time. Shortly after Alex's death, our long-time and beloved dog, Samantha, had died. Neither of us were in the mood for a new pet when a calico cat came to our house with stubborn determination to remain with us. Our children suggested, "Maybe Alex and Samantha sent her."

Humming birds and butterflies, often associated with rebirth, are frequent visitors to our backyard. They often come right up and hover in front of me, as if in greeting. Their nearness triggers my strongest memories of Alex. At such times I can still see Alex's face, hear his voice.

Although these memories still remain precious to me, I learned soon after his death that family, friends, and acquaintances did not want to hear about them. Our death denying society wants silence from the suffering and sorrowing. As Anna Quindlen states, "Grief remains one of the few things that has the power to silence us. It is a whisper in the world and a clamor within. More than sex, more than faith, even more than its usher death, grief is unspoken, publicly ignored except for those moments at the funeral that are over too quickly . . ." [2, p. 29].

Many people assured me that I "would grow" from my grief experience. I was not interested in growth. Only years later, after much study and living through my grief, am I willing to accede to the possibility that grief holds the potential for enrichment and sensitivity. I finally can appreciate the following, printed in a grief seminar brochure.

Grief and mourning can become:
a stagnant pond—or a river
a cave—or a tunnel
a place—or a journey[1]

Converting my pond to a river, dark cave to a tunnel, and sorrow to a journey has not occurred in a linear fashion. My mourning continues to be an ongoing and uneven struggle. Particularly in the early years, brief glimmers of optimism were eclipsed by despair and depression. Anger usually overruled logic. Irritation displaced peace. I wandered between shock, depression, anger, irritation, and often total fatigue.

When feeling totally bereft, I doubted my intuitive belief that I could survive. My training and experience as a nurse had taught me the need to heed and endure my chaotic feelings. But making choices on how to deal with those feelings often seemed beyond my immediate strength and ability. Attempts to be patient with myself were not always successful.

Prevailing societal attitudes frequently made choices difficult. Distractions were the usual offerings of the world that wanted me to be stoic and "take it well." Psychology tells us, however, we must face, explore, and ventilate our feelings. That dichotomy made me realize my own accountability and responsibilities.

Evaluating my personal myths—my self-script—helped me make a conscious confirmation of them, and then to choose to overcome the destructive ones. I discovered I was not immune to many traditional ideas about how one should grieve:

- bury my feelings
- grieve alone
- just give it time
- regret the past (different, better, more)

---

[1] "When a Baby Dies, Helping Family Grieve," Marilyn Gryte, RN, MS, Lecturer, Carondelet Management Institute, Phoenix, AZ, September 17, 1992.

• be seen and not heard (appear in public to assure others that I was O.K., but don't discuss my grief).

In *Seven Choices,* Elizabeth Harper Neeld discusses choosing to experience, embrace our pain, to express grief fully, to suffer and endure, to take action, to look honestly, and to continue to make choices [3, pp. 6-8]. Through this process she believes one can regain balance in life and thus gain freedom from grief's domination.

Neeld's emphasis on choosing struck a chord with me, and I realized the responsibility for the shape and form of my future would be up to me. Engulfed by my grief, making choices seemed beyond my capacity until I realized that allowing myself to experience the full impact of my loss involved a choice in itself.

I slowly began to look at my physical and emotional requirements. I began to realize the wisdom of making healthy rather than destructive choices about my diet, exercise, and even rest and sleep. While tempted to try and anesthetize myself with drugs or alcohol when sleep was difficult, I could choose to read or meditate instead.

Finding acceptable means of transforming my complicated feelings into something manageable, something that would give me an "ongoing resource for healing" [4, p. 28], proved daunting. Crying and screaming felt like the most immediate and satisfactory method. Expressing my anguish in such a manner, although feeling legitimate, was not always appreciated by those who happened to be in the vicinity. Still, I understood the wisdom of Feinstein and Mayo, who said, "In the alchemy of transmuting grief and anguish to wisdom and creativity, *emotional expression* is a central activity. *Psychological discharge, ventilation,* or *catharsis* are terms for describing the core emotional process in conscious, ritualized grieving" [5, p. 128].

My need for more sociably acceptable and creative methods dealing with my emotions led to a number of personal rituals. Daily rites were the most useful during the early stages of my mourning. One of those activities included what I call "grieving on schedule." The constant fatigue and distress of grief often comes from the struggle to "be strong, brave, and not break down." When crying, a natural physical response to loss,[2] is suppressed, exhaustion ensues. Setting a time every day to remember and to grieve freed me to approach my normal routines. The time I set aside was a regularly planned interval undisturbed by phone calls, guests, or chores—a time inviolate—a time that respected my needs. Often I spent, and still do spend, this time writing, listening to music, or reading.

Greeting card rituals became treacherous, however. The first card that came from Alex's family following his death was a Grandparent's Day card signed "Curtis and Stephanie." Who are these people, I thought? My head knew, of course, but not my heart. Without Alex's name, the salutation did not make sense. I also had difficulty remembering how many cards to buy, or for whom. Finally someone suggested I buy one for Alex also, and that helped. I have the same problem when answering "how many grandchildren do you have?" For me, the answer must always include Alex.

Writing became my salvation. By putting my anguish into words, I could start to give it new shape and meaning while affirming my feelings. Writing out my frustrations, depression, and despair helped me embrace my life with all its sorrows and contradictions. I found Gabriele Rico's statement true that, "When we hurt, a natural response is to blame people or events *out there* for our pain. But there is another way, and that is to respond metaphorically—that is, to use language and its emotional grammar to express our feelings in words that transform the pain into images" [6, pp. 121-122].

In the privacy of my journal I explored the intricacies of my suffering and symbolically screamed in pain rather than ". . . be mute in the face of devastating pain and let the grief recycle itself inside of me" [6, p. 145]. In that safe place I started to manage my pain and despair through language, and began to see myself and my grief in a new light.

---

[2] http.www.geisinger.edu/ghs/pubtips/P/THEPURPOSEOFTEARS.htm

Describing my pain and fear helped me start to control it. With that power came the possibility I could even give it a voice and ask it what it wanted, or what it had to teach—what it needed to heal and how long that might take. I agree with Gabriele Rico that "If speaking and writing involve the grammar of language, I believe that we can also speak of an emotional grammar—a grammar reflecting the silent language of the heart" [6, p. 100].

Sydney Metrick also suggests, "Get to know your pain. Understand it. Find out what happens when you interact with it" [4, p. 24], even though that pain probably feels like a stalking stranger. She also suggests describing and understanding pain through writing, but further suggests the more active methods of drawing, painting, or sculpting it. A sculpture class I took for several semesters offered the opportunity to express myself in several mediums. Eventually I settled on working with clay as I find the manipulation of that material to be extremely satisfying.

Another important and consistent method for coping with my life problems has been to take some sort of action. A major choice of action has been to write this book. Some of my other choices of action since Alex died have included:

- Writing letters, making phone calls, and handling insurance problems that my children felt needed to be done, but felt they were not able to do.
- Talking frequently by telephone to David and Andrea and taking frequent trips to their home.
- Sending cards, letters, and sometimes small gifts to my surviving grandchildren.
- Sending cards, letters, and sometimes flowers to David and Andrea on special days, especially on Alex's birthday and death date.
- Doing research on the genetic defect, x-linked lymphoproliferative disease, that took Alex's life.
- Doing research on grief issues and sharing information with my grieving children.
- Visiting and attending grief groups.

- Developing a grandparent survey.
- Taking college classes that interested me.
- Doing volunteer work.

Choosing to no longer participate in some activities has also been important. Through that type of choice, I have received the benefit of releasing the tension of trying to be what others want me to be.

Such mundane activities as watching sports on TV and going to ball-games, while perhaps not as constructive as others, nonetheless help by giving me moments of distraction from my grief. Choosing regular companionship with supportive individuals, whether family, friends, therapist, or in grief groups, has been beneficial also.

These choices and activities helped me find and develop my new role—who I had become as a bereaved grandparent.

Other grieving grandparents with whom I have corresponded agree that the relationship between themselves and their child, the parent of the dead grandchild, can be severely strained from such a loss. All relationships require time and energy, but following the death of a child the demands on grandparent and adult child can be enormous.

My son, his family, and I have struggled to re-define our relationships since Alex's death. Sometimes we have been successful, other times less so. Always it has seemed a daunting task. Each of us had our own unique response to the loss of Alex, and also have dealt with that loss in our individual manner and time. Those differences in personalities and grief processes have created, from time to time, considerable frustration, confusion, and added pain.

To express my grief and needs with any authenticity, I learned, required a great deal of courage. Sometimes even more courage was necessary to give physical and emotional support to my son and his family. I chose to be available to David and Andrea and their family as often as possible and particularly when they asked for help.

Slowly a reconciliation with my dual loss has come about as I developed new ways of living. My priorities are different now. Many things that had previously seemed important no longer disturb or occupy me. As someone who had lived most of her life feeling she must "be all things to all people," I have learned the valuable lesson of spending more time doing those things that I really want to do and less on those that I previously thought I "ought" to do. My selection of friends is now those who enrich my life rather than take energy from it.

After being raised in the Protestant faith and continuing to attend church regularly as an adult, since Alex's death my spiritual focus has shifted. My belief that there exists a unifying force in the universe has not changed, but I no longer find usefulness in religion dogma. I now strive to maintain a spiritual center that Flach has described as ". . . what you do well within the framework of a system of values that you respect . . ." [8, p. 254]. One of the anchors now when life's problems assail me is the knowledge that, "It could be worse, or worse things could happen."

It has been ten years since Alex died. That cruel moment changed me; whether for the better or for the worse, I am not the one to say. What I am aware of, however, is that my patience with people who are suffering has increased while my tolerance for those that are inconsiderate and self-centered has shortened.

My respect for the mystery of life and death has deepened. That didn't happen all at once, but rather through the choices I have made in finding my way through grief. They are choices that, without a doubt, would have been different had Alex lived. They have not been necessarily the right choices, or the wrong choices, just my choices, my road.

> I shall be telling this with a sigh
> Somewhere ages and ages hence:
> Two roads diverged in a wood, and I—
> I took the one less traveled by,
> And that has made all the difference [9, p. 105].

I will continue risking, loving, and losing. I still cry about losing Alex and the consequences of his death on my child and his family. The terrible wound I suffered when he died will remain, in some fashion, for the rest of my life. Therefore, I still hurt from time to time. That does not mean that I have not come to some reconciliation of my loss. Alex now lives in my heart.

REFERENCES

1. J. Tatelbaum, *The Courage to Grieve,* Harper & Row Publishers, New York, 1980.
2. A. Quindlen, The Often-Invisible Burden of Survivors, *U.S. Catholic,* July 1994 (reprinted from the New York Times Company).
3. E. H. Neeld, *Seven Choices,* Clarkson N. Potter, Inc., New York, 1990.
4. S. B. Metrick, *Crossing the Bridge: Creating Ceremonies for Grieving and Healing from Life's Losses,* Celestial Arts, Berkeley, California, 1994.
5. D. Feinstein and P. E. Mayo, *Rituals for Living & Dying,* HarperCollins, San Francisco, 1990.
6. G. L. Rico, *Pain and Possibility: Writing Your Way Through Personal Crisis,* Jeremy P. Tarcher, Inc., Los Angeles, 1991.
7. F. Flach, *Resilience,* Fawcett Columbine, New York, 1988.
8. "The Road Not Taken," *The Poetry of Robert Frost,* E. C. Lathem (ed.), Holt, Rinehart & Winston, New York, 1969.

EPILOGUE

A DNA analysis done on members of Alex's family following his death revealed a 99 percent probability that Curtis had the defective gene that causes x-linked lymphoproliferative disease (Duncan Syndrome). The results of that analysis were not available until after Curtis was hospitalized in May of 1990. Our mourning for Alex became protracted and complicated with the possibility that Curtis might not survive the lymphomatoid granulomatosis (a rare affliction associated with x-linked lymphoproliferative syndrome) that was essentially overgrowing his lungs.

Curtis underwent a little over a year of chemotherapy and steroid therapy. As of this writing he has finished high school and appears healthy, despite chronic health problems. He remains susceptible to the Epstein-Barr virus that causes mononucleosis and that caused Alex's death. Curtis takes daily anti-viral medication and a monthly IV injection of an immune booster.

Another son, Landen, was born into the family two years after Alex's death. Since the genetic defect that causes x-linked lymphoproliferative syndrome affects males and is carried by females, David and Andrea made a hard decision to continue the pregnancy. Further DNA testing following Landen's birth found both Stephanie and Landen to be free of the genetic defect.

Stephanie has been an active and winning participant in beauty contests since she was six months old. Her parents found pageant activity helped distract them from their pain, but more importantly helped them focus attention on their baby daughter. Stephanie has taken lessons in singing, gymnastics, and dance, and consequently has developed great poise and confidence for her age.

Landen is a very active and beautiful child who enjoys gym, baseball, soccer, ice and roller skating, and rowdy play.

Somehow life has gone on—we have survived—altered forever by our loss, but a family struggling to communicate, love, and enjoy the world around us.

Appendix I

SELECTED POEMS

Solace for my breaking heart I found in many different and often surprising places: special people, nature, animals, music, books, and poetry. Following are a few of the poems that have touched and supported me through my grief journey.

Several of the poems were sent to me by friends or family. "Little Boy Blue" is a poem that I read and loved as a child. Two of the poems were written by members of my wonderful writer's group, without which this entire project would never have been completed.

The first poem comes from a book, with a publishing date of 1894, belonging to my mother-in-law. Where, when, and how she obtained it I have no idea, for it came to me after her death. What I found particularly appealing and remarkably moving about this poem was not only the poignant sentiment, but the realization of its utter timelessness—feelings expressed over a century ago speak eloquently to our grief from the loss of a child today.

My Little Boy That Died

Look at his pretty face for just one minute,
His braided frock, his dainty buttoned shoes,
His firm-shut hand, the favorite plaything in it
And tell me, mothers, was't not hard to lose
    And miss him from my side—
    My little boy that died?

How many another boy as dear and charming,
His father's hope, his mother's one delight,
Slips through strange sickness, all fear disarming,
And lives a long, long life in parents' sight!
    Mine was so short a pride!
    And then my poor boy died?

I see him rocking on his wooden charger;
I hear him pattering through the house all day;
I watch his great blue eyes grow large and larger,
Listening to stories, whether grave or gay,
    Told at the bright fireside—
    So dark now, since he died.

But yet I often think my boy is living,
As living as my other children are;
When good-night kisses I all around am giving,
I keep one for him though he is so far.
    Can a mere grave divide
    Me from him, though he died?

So while I come and plant it o'er with daisies,
(Nothing but childish daisies, all year round),
Continually God's hand the curtain raises,
And I can hear his merry voice's sound
    And feel him at my side—
    My little boy that died.

Dinah Muloch-Craik
Gems of Poetry
Rhodes & McClure Pub. Co., Chicago
p. 280, 1894

Little Boy Blue

The little toy dog is covered with dust,
    But sturdy and stanch he stands;
And the little toy soldier is red with rust,
    And his musket molds in his hands.

Time was when the little toy dog was new
    And the soldier was passing fair,
And that was the time when our Little Boy Blue
    Kissed them and put them there.

"Now don't you go till I come," he said,
    "And don't you make any noise!"
So toddling off to his trundle-bed
    He dreamed of the pretty toys.
And as he was dreaming, an angel song
    Awakened our Little Boy Blue—
Oh, the years are many, the years are long
    But the little toy friends are true.

Aye, faithful to Little Boy Blue they stand,
    Each in the same old place,
Awaiting the touch of a little hand,
    And the smile of a little face.
And they wonder, as waiting these long years through,
    In the dust of that little chair,
What has become of our Little Boy Blue
    Since he kissed them and put them there.

Eugene Field
A Treasury of the Familiar
Consolidated Book Publishers, Chicago
p. 603, 1944

Grief

Grief feels like a cave,
an aimless groping
into a black, deepening void.
Into your hand I press
the only candle I have,
a message
to flicker in the darkness of your soul:
Grief feels like a cave, but it
is not a cave.
Grief is a tunnel, a journey.

The blackness is the same.
The only difference is Hope.

Marilyn Gryte, RN, MS
Dear Parents: A Collection of Letters to Bereaved Parents.
Centering: Omaha, NE, © 1989

Do not stand at my grave and weep
I am not there. I do not sleep.
I am a thousand winds that blow
I am the diamond glint on snow.
I am the sunlight on ripened grain
I am the gentle autumn rain.
When you wake in the morning hush
I am the swift, uplifting rush
    of quiet birds in circling flight.
I am the soft starlight at night.
Do not stand at my grave and weep.
I am not there. I do not sleep.

Author Unknown

Excerpt from:
Elegy for Philippe-Maguilen
October 17, 1958-June 7, 1981

. . . "And I said "No!" to the doctor. "My son is not dead,
    it is impossible"
Pardon me, Lord, and sweep away my blasphemy, but
    it is impossible.
No, no! Those who are coddled by the gods do not
    die so young."

By Leopold-Seder Senghor
Former President of Senegal
(Quoted from *Recovering from the Loss of a Child*
by Katherine Fair Donnelly
Macmillan, New York, 1982)

Two Houses

This is my grieving house.
Like the Moon Houses of my mothers,
I withdraw here into open space filled
with comfortable red light to be apart.

It is like crawling inside an egg,
It is like being a seed aware
of itself rotting in the ground
but not understanding the strange new
shoots sprouting from its sagging wounds.

When I am inside my grieving house
I paint myself red for protection.
I practice parthenogenesis:
I give birth to myself.

The long deep love labor
of a screaming belly,
a belly in the brain,
a belly in the soul,
permitting my body
to be broken
among earth's grave
bone.

I swim in inner sea water
though I do not know how to swim.

Come near only if you are willing
to dye your skin with your own blood
and lie with me face down on the ground.

Later, we shall move out
to join the feast
in our common house of healing.

Alla Renee Bozarth, Ph.D.
Life is Goodbye, Life is Hello, p. 175, Copyright 1982, 1986
Reprinted by permission of Hazelden Foundation
Center City, MN

Memory builds a little pathway
That goes winding through my heart.
It's a lovely, quiet, gentle trail
From other things apart . . .
I only meet when traveling there
The people I like best,
For this road I call "Remembrance"
Is hidden from the rest

I always know I'll find you
In my memory rendezvous,
For I keep a special meeting place
Especially for you.

Helen Steiner Rice
Used with permission of the *Helen Steiner Rice Foundation*
Suite 2100, Atrium Two, 221 East Fourth Street
Cincinnati, OH, 45202

Why?

At his father's deathbed
my son's question comes
raw as a fresh wound
ancient as the sorrow of Job.

The question circles, persists
like an insistent insect
becomes all that exists
until we are deafened
made mute
immobilized
by the buzzing.

Others are tantalized
by such questions
collect them like butterflies
impale them on theories
categorize in schisms
press them in their books.

Skeptics puzzle
over fluttering wings
stand hypnotized
by shape, line, color.

I brush aside their buzzing.
for me
all is mystery
transcendence
awesome flight.

Even in this room of shadows
my son's bright hair
catches the light.

Lorene Hoover
(Unpublished, used by permission of the author)

Stars Are Angels

I looked at the stars in the sky one night
And saw a blessed, heavenly sight
When once composed I settle myself
Put doubtful feelings on the shelf
A blissful vision then appeared
Soft words of angels, true and clear.
You'd think it was a movie screen
With sacred music pure—serene
Angel wings etched in each star
They were so near, and yet so far
One touched me gently with its wing
And offered angel songs to sing.
"Thou art a heavenly, living soul
Infinite Spirit is our goal."
And when the song was done
Me and the Angels had tons of fun
We played Peek-a-Boo and games like that
With angelic stories as we sat.

Soon it was time for the Angels to leave
A farewell embrace did I receive
I gazed at the stars and what did I see?
A sky of Angels looking down on me.

RaQuel Love
(Unpublished, used by permission of the author)

After A While

After a while you learn the subtle difference
Between holding a hand and chaining a soul,
And you learn that love doesn't mean leaning,
And company doesn't mean security.

And you begin to learn that kisses aren't contracts,
And presents aren't promises,
And you begin to accept your defeats
With your head up and your eyes open
With the grace of a woman, not the grief of a child.

And you learn to build all your roads
On today because tomorrow's ground
Is too uncertain for plans, and futures have
A way of falling down in mid-flight.

After a while you learn that even sunshine
Burns if you get too much.

So you plant your own garden and decorate
Your own soul, instead of waiting
For someone to bring you flowers.

And you learn that you really can endure . . .
That you really are strong
And you really do have worth.

And you learn and learn . . .
With every good-bye you learn

Veronica A Shoffstall
© 1971

Beyond Dream's Edge

Three new children play tonight
In a land beyond dream's edge.
Instead of sand, they play with stardust,
Getting glitter sprinkles on their hands.

Instead of coloring books,
They color rainbows
For God to place in the sky,
His promise to us below.

Instead of jumping rope,
They jump strands of sunlight,
Braided strong by His might,
Forever shining bright.

Instead of riding bikes,
They spread their wings
And fly to distant stars,
As all the angels sing.

Instead of snow slopes,
They slide down moonbeams,
Iridescent glowing streams,
Landing in heavenly green.

Instead of TV,
They watch sunrises, sunsets,
And all that transpires in between,
Secure that God knows best.

Instead of playing ball,
They catch the stars
Before they fall,
Loving the wonder of it all.

Instead of bounding on beds,
They bounce on clouds,
Their laughter echoes about,
Just beyond dream's edge.

We meet at night in prayer.
I quietly wait to see them there,
Golden halos on their heads,
In a land beyond dream's edge.

Debbie Dickinson
Breeavement Magazine,
5125 N. Union Blvd. Suite #4
Colorado Springs, CO 80918-2056

In Memory of Our Beloved Children

In the rising of the sun
   and in its going down:
      we remember them.
In the blowing of the wind
   and in the chill of winter:
      we remember them.
In the opening of buds
   and in the warmth of summer:
      we remember them.
In the rustling of leaves
   and the beauty of autumn:
      we remember them.
In the beginning of the year
   and in when it ends:
      we remember them.
For we are weary
   and in need of strength:
      we remember them.
When we are lost
   and sick at heart:
      we remember them.
When we have joys we
   yearn to share:
      we remember them.

So long as we live
They too shall live
For they are now a part of us:
  As we remember them.

Jewish Prayer for Children
Gates of Prayer, Reform Judaism Prayer Book
Materials from *Gates of Prayer* are copyright by the
Central Conference of American Rabbis
and are produced by permission

The Hour of Lead

This is the hour of lead
Remembered if outlived
As freezing persons
  recollect
The snow—
First chill, then stupor, then
The letting go.

Emily Dickinson
Excerpt of poem 1st published in 1891.
The Complete Poems of Emily Dickinson
Thomas H. Johnson, ed., Little, Brown and Company
Boston, New York, London, Toronto, pp. 161-162, 1960

Appendix II

RESOURCES

Many organizations offer grief assistance on national, state, and local levels. Most of these organizations have Web sites on the Internet which is an excellent method of accessing information about them. For those who do not have personal access to the Internet, most libraries offer that service.

The following is a partial list of associations and organizations that offer support and education to those suffering the loss of a loved one.

American Association of Suicidology AAS
4201 Connecticut Ave, NW
Suite 310
Washington, DC 20008
E-mail: none
Fax: (202) 237-2282
URL: http://www.cyberpsych.org/aas.htm

American Suicide Foundation (ASF)
Address: 120 Wall Street, 22nd Floor
New York, NY 10005
Phone: (800) ASF-4042; (212) 410-1111
Fax: (212) 269-7259
E-mail: none
URL: www.asfnet.org

American Sudden Infant Death Syndrome (SIDS) Institute
6065 Roswell Road, Suite 876
Atlanta, GA 30328
Phone: (404) 843-1030
Fax: (404) 843-0577
E-mail: prevent@sids.org
URL: http://www.sids.org/

Association for Death Education and Counseling
638 Prospect Avenue
Hartford, CT 06105-4250
Phone: (860) 586-7503
Fax: (860) 586-7550
E-mail: info@adec.org
URL: http://www.adec.org/

Compassion Books
477 Hannah Branch Road
Burnsville, NC 28714
Phone: (704) 675-5909
Fax: (740) 675-9687
E-mail: Heal2grow@aol.com
URL: http://www.compassionbooks.com

The Centering Corporation
1531 Saddle Creek Rd.
Omaha, NE 68104
E-mail: J1200@aol.com

The Candlelighters Childhood Cancer Foundation
7910 Woodmont Ave., Suite 460
Bethesda, MD 20814-3015
Phone: 1-800-366-2223
        301-657-8401
Fax: 301-718-2686
E-mail: info@candlelighters.org
URL: http://www.candlelighters.org/#what

The Compassionate Friends
The Compassionate Friends is a national nonprofit, self-help support organization which offers friendship and understanding to families who are grieving the death of a child of any age, from any cause.

P.O. Box 3696
Oak Brook, IL 60522-3696
Phone: (630) 990-0010
E-mail: tcf_national@prodigy.com
URL: http://www.jjt.com/~tcf_national/

Hospice Foundation of America
Suite 300, 2001 S Street NW
Washington, DC 20009
Phone: (202) 638-5312 / (800) 854-3402
Fax: (202) 638-5312
E-mail: hospicefdn@charitiesusa.com
URL: http://www.hospicefoundation.org

National Hospice Organization
1901 North Moore Street, Suite 901
Arlington, VA 22209-1714
Phone: (703) 243-5900
Fax: (703) 525-5762
http://www.nho.org/

Parents of Murdered Children, Inc.
100 East Eighth Street, B-41
Cincinnati, OH 45202
Phone: (513) 721-5683
Fax: (513) 345-4489
E-mail: NatlPOMC@aol.com
URL: http://www.metroguide.com/pomc/

Mothers Against Drunk Driving (MADD)
511 E. John Carpenter Frwy. #700
Irving, TX 75062

Phone: (214) 744-6233
E-mail: Info@madd.org
URL: http://www.madd.org/

RTS Bereavement Services (Miscarriage, ectopic pregnancy, stillbirth, newborn death)
1910 South Avenue
La Crosse, WI 54601
Phone: (800) 362-9567 Ext. 4747
Fax: (608) 791-5137

SANDS (Stillbirth and Neonatal Death Support)
P.O. Box 302
Chelsea VIC 3196
Support: (03) 9773 0221
Phone: (03) 9773 0228
Fax: (03) 9773 0226
E-mail: info@sandsvic.org.au
URL: http://www.sandsvic.org.au/index.htm

Besides the above organizations, many sites on the Internet offer only online services such as grief information, counseling, book lists, resource lists, chat rooms, and memorial sites. Online sites also offer assistance for bereavement due to unusual diseases and circumstances. Three of these online only services are:

The Grief Recovery Institute
E-mail: gri@grief-recovery.com
http://www.grief-recovery.com/

Grief, Loss and Recovery
http://www.erichad.com/grief/

Ray of Hope
http://www.valinet.com/~kevlynn/

BIBLIOGRAPHY
(References Not Cited in Text)

Achterberg, Jeanne, Barbara Dossey, and Leslie Kolkmeir, *Rituals of Healing: Using Imagery for Health and Wellness,* Bantam Books, New York, 1994.

Albertson, Sandra Hayward, *Endings & Beginnings,* Random House, New York, 1980.

Baranell, Sylvia, *When a Child Dies,* Thetford Press Limited, Thetford, Norfork, 1984.

Bernstein, Judith, *When the Bough Breaks,* Andrews and McMeel, Kansas City, Missouri, 1997.

Biegert, John G., *When Death Has Touched Your Life,* Pilgrim Press, New York, 1981.

Bode, Janet, *Death Is Hard To Live With,* Delacorte Press, New York, 1993.

Bonheim, Jalaja, *The Serpent and the Wave: A Guide to Movement Meditation,* Celestial Arts, Berkeley, California, 1992.

Childs-Gowell, Elaine, *Good Grief Rituals: Tools for Healing,* Station Hill Press, New York, 1992.

Colgrove, Melba, Harold H. Bloomfield, and Peter McWilliams, *How to Survive the Loss of a Love,* Bantam Books, New York, 1981.

Crenshaw, David A., *Bereavement: Counseling the Grieving Throughout the Life Cycle,* The Continuum, New York, 1990.

Crider, Tom, *Give Sorrow Words: A Father's Passage Through Grief,* Algonquin Books, Chapel Hill, North Carolina, 1996.

Davidson, Glen W., *Understanding Mourning: A Guide for Those Who Grieve,* Augusburg Publishing House, Minneapolis, 1984.

Deits, Bob, *Life After Loss,* Fisher Books, Tucson, Arizona, 1988.

Diaz, Adriana, *Freeing the Creative Spirit,* HarperCollins, San Francisco, 1992.

Dickens, Monica, *Miracles of Courage,* Dodd, Mead & Company, New York, 1985.

Donnelly, Nina Herrmann, *I Never Know What to Say,* Ballantine Books, New York, 1987.

Eadie, Betty J., *Embraced By The Light,* Gold Leaf Press, Placerville, California, 1992.

Finkbeiner, Ann K., *After the Death of a Child,* The Free Press, New York, 1996.

Fitzgerald, Helen, *The Mourning Handbook,* Simon & Schuster, New York, 1994.

Frankl, Viktor E., *Man's Search for Meaning,* Simon & Schuster, New York, 1984.

Grof, Stanslav/Christina, *Beyond Death,* Thames and Hudson Ltd., London, 1980.

James, John and Frank Cherry, *Grief Recovery Handbook,* Harper & Row, New York, 1988.

Kübler-Ross, Elisabeth, *On Children and Death,* Macmillan, New York, 1983.

Kushner, Harold S., *Who Needs God,* Summit Books, New York, 1989.

Kushner, Harold S., *When Bad Things Happen to Good People,* Avon Books, New York, 1981.

Levine, Stephen, *Healing Into Life & Death,* Anchor Press/ Doubleday, New York, 1987.

Lewis, C. S., *A Grief Observed,* Seaburg Press, New York, 1961.

Lightner, Candy and Nancy Hathaway, *Giving Sorrow Words,* Warner Books, New York, 1990.

Lord, Janice Harris, *Beyond Sympathy,* Pathfinder, Ventura, California, 1988.

Manning, Doug, *Comforting Those Who Grieve,* Harper & Row, San Francisco, 1985.

Manning, Doug, *Don't Take My Grief Away,* Harper & Row, New York, 1962.

Moffat, Mary Jane (ed.), *In the Midst of Winter,* Vintage Books, New York, 1992.

Morse, Melvin with Paul Perry, *Closer to the Light,* Villard Books, New York, 1990.

O'Connor, Nancy, *Letting Go With Love: The Grieving Process,* La Mariposa Press, Tucson, Arizona, 1984.

Osgood, Judy (ed.), *Meditations for Bereaved Parents,* Gilgal Publications, Sunriver, Oregon, 1983.
Parrish-Harra, Reverend Carol W., *The New Age Handbook on Death and Dying,* IBS Press, Santa Monica, California, 1982.
Ponzetti, Jr., James J. and Mary A. Johnson, The Forgotten Grievers: Grandparent's Reactions to the Death of a Grandchild, *Death Studies,* March/April 1991.
Raphael, Beverley, *The Anatomy of Bereavement,* Basic Books, New York, 1983.
Rosen, Helen, *Unspoken Grief: Coping with Childhood Sibling Loss,* D. C. Heath and Company, Lexington, Massachusetts, 1986.
Ryan, Regina Sara, *No Child in My Life,* Stillpoint, Walpole, New Hampshire, 1993.
Schmidt, Judith Sara, *How to Cope with Grief,* Ballantine Books, New York (Blue Cliff Ed.), 1989.
Siegel, Bernie S., *Love, Medicine and Miracles,* Harper & Row, New York, 1986.
Simos, Bertha G., *A Time to Grieve: Loss as a Universal Human Experience,* Family Service Association of America, New York, 1979.
Singer, Lilly, Margaret Sirot, and Susan Rodd, *Beyond Loss,* E. P. Dutton, New York, 1988.
Spiegel, Yorick, *The Grief Process: Analysis & Counseling,* Abingdon Press, Nashville, 1973.
Staudacher, Carol, *Beyond Grief,* New Harbinger Publications, Inc., Oakland, California, 1987.
Staudacher, Carol, *Men and Grief,* New Harbinger Publications, Inc., Oakland, California, 1991.
Staudacher, Carol, *A Time to Grieve: Meditations for Healing After the Death of a Loved One,* HarperCollins, New York, 1994.
Stearns, Ann Kaiser, *Coming Back: Rebuilding Lives After Crisis and Loss,* Ballantine Books, New York, 1988.
Tengbom, Mildred, *Grief for a Season,* Bethany House Publishers, Minneapolis, Minnesota, 1989.
Van Vechten, B. D., and Robert Veninga, *A Gift of Hope: How We Survive Our Tragedies,* Little, Brown & Company, Boston, 1985.
Volkan, Vamik D. and Elizabeth Zintl, *Life After Loss,* Macmillan, New York, 1993.
Wasserman, Selma, *The Long Distance Grandmother,* Hartley & Marks, Point Roberts, Washington, 1988.

Westburg, Granger, *Good Grief,* Harper & Row, New York, 1962.

Wolfelt, Alan, *A Child's View of Grief,* Service Corporation International, Denver, 1990.

Wolterstoff, Nicholas, *Lament For a Son,* Wm. B. Eerdmans, Grand Rapids, Michigan, 1987.

Yancy, Phillip, *Where is God When it Hurts,* Harper Paperbacks, New York, 1977.

Zunin, Leonard M. and Hilary Stanton Zunin, *The Art of Condolence,* Harper Perennial, New York, 1991.

Index

Andreae, Christine, 12
Auden, W. H., 13

Beck, Renee & S. B. Metrick,
  76
Bereavement Magazine, 66, 79
Bozarth, Alla Renee, 43-44
Burial, 74

Cadoff, Jennifer, 65
Compassionate Friends, 22,
  70, 86
Courage, 93-94
Cramer, Kathryn, 23
Crying, 32-33, 44, 98
Cunningham, Ginny, 30

Divorce (*see* Marital Conflicts)
Donations, 75
Donnelly, Katherine Fair,
  29-30, 40
Duncan's syndrome
  (*see* X-linked
  lymphoproliferative
  disease)

Elkins, Rita, 50
Epstein-Barr virus, 8-9
Ericsson, Stephanie, 29

Feinstein, David & P. Mayo, 97
Field, Eugene, 11
Fischoff, Joseph, 23-24
Flach, Frederic, 45-46, 101
Friends and family, 21
Frost, Robert, 101
Funeral, 94

Gerner, Margaret H., 26, 55
Grandparents
  as role models, 58
  evaluating our strengths,
    45-46
  feelings of powerlessness, 12
  physical needs, 32
  returning to routines, 16
  taking action, 99
Grief
  books and articles on, 25
  influencing factors for
    children, 68
  issues, 27

[Grief]
myths about children's,
66-67
stages and phases, 34-35
support groups, 22-24
time will heal, 19, 33, 90
usual reaction to, 37-38
unevenness of, 38
Grimes, Laura, 83, 91
Gryte, Marilyn, 24, 86, 96
George, Elizabeth, 21, 27, 81,
84

Help
practical for our children, 57
Houghton, Ray, 22, 59

Irving, John, 13

James, John W., 65
Jewish Prayer for Children, 73
Johnson, Sherry, 26
Journaling (*see* Writing)

Keen, Sam, 78
Knapp, Ronald, 31
Kolf, June Cerza, 22
Kreis, Bernadine, 73
Kübler-Ross, Elisabeth,
34, 67

Letters, 77, 99
Linn, Erin, 89
Listening, 22, 59-60
Loss
missing parts to, 13
reactions to, 37

Magical thinking, 64
Martial conflicts, 39
Metrick, Sydney Barbara, 86, 97
Memorials
private, 79
Memories, 80
Merchant, Jane, 19
McMurtry, Larry, 17
Music, 76
Myths
about children's grief, 66-67
personal, 96

Neeld, Elizabeth Harper, 97
Nelson, G. Lynn, 3
Nerken, Ira, 83
New Song, 24, 67-68

Pain, 44
Paretsky, Sara, 31
Personal needs
asking for help, 52-53
body awareness, 49
educating ourselves, 53
prioritizing, 50
social/emotional support, 52
Personal rituals, 78
Personal timeline, 46-47
Physical needs
exercise, 48
nutrition, 48
sleep/relaxation, 49
Ponzetti James, 26, 37, 81

Rando, Therese A., 26-27, 34,
36-40, 43, 59
Rico, Gabriele, 45, 98-99
Rosof, Barbara, 81
Roth, Deborah, 84, 91

Sadness, 30-31
Sanders, Catherine M., 73
Schafer, Don, 68
Schiff, Harriet Sarnoff, 25
Seibert, Dinah, 64
Shakespeare, 2
Shaw, George Bernard, 67
Spirituality/Religion, 50-51

Tatelbaum, Judy, 93
Touching, 58
Things to remember, 87-88

Questionnaire, 25
Quindlen, Ann, 95

Viorst, Judith, 18-19
Video, 70, 76

Wolfelt, Alan, 24, 30, 63, 65-68
Worden, William, 35-36, 39-40
Wordsworth, William, 5
Writing, 43-45, 79, 81, 98-99

X-linked lymphoproliferative
disease, 8

Other Books of Interest in the Death, Value and Meaning Series

Series Editor: John D. Morgan

The Magical Thoughts of Grieving Children: Treating Children
with Complicated Mourning and Advice for Parents
By James A. Fogarty, Ed.D.

We Love You Matty: Meeting Death with Faith
By Tad Dunne, Ph.D.

Death Without Notice
By Sandra Helene Straub

Meeting the Needs of Our Clients Creatively:
The Impact of Art and Culture on Caregiving
Editor: John D. Morgan

Grief and the Healing Arts: Creativity as Therapy
Editor: Sandra L. Bertman

When a Child Has Been Murdered:
Ways You Can Help the Grieving Parents
By Bonnie Hunt Conrad

The Death of an Adult Child:
A Book for and About Bereaved Parents
By Jeanne Webster Blank

When Dreams Don't Work: Professional Caregivers and Burnout
By Ronna Jevne and Donna Reilly Williams

Heavenly Hurts: Surviving AIDS Related Deaths and Losses
By Sandra Jacoby Klein

All Kinds of Love: Experiencing Hospice
By Carolyn Jaffe and Carol H. Ehrlich

Readings in Thanatology
Editor: John D. Morgan

Mending the Torn Fabric: For Those Who Grieve
and Those Who Want to Help Them
By Sarah Brabant

Widower: When Men Are Left Alone
By Scott Campbell and Phyllis R. Silverman

Awareness of Mortality
Editor: Jeffrey Kauffman

Ethical Issues in the Care of the Dying and Bereaved Aged
Editor: John D. Morgan

Fading Away: The Experience of Transition in Families with
Terminal Illness
Editors: Betty Davies, Joanne Chekryn Reimer,
Pamela Brown and Nola Martens

Last Rites: The Work of the Modern Funeral Director
By: Glennys Howarth

Perspectives on College Student Suicide
By Ralph L. V. Rickgarn

What Will We Do?
Preparing a School Community to Cope with Crises
Editor: Robert G. Stevenson

Personal Care in an Impersonal World:
A Multidimensional Look at Bereavement
Editor: John D. Morgan

Death and Spirituality
Editor: Kenneth J. Doka with John D. Morgan

Spiritual, Ethical and Pastoral Aspects
of Death and Bereavement
Editors: Gerry R. Cox and Ronald J. Fundis

Greeting the Angels: An Imaginal View of the Mourning Process
By Greg Mogenson

Beyond the Innocence of Childhood – 3 Volume Set
Editors: David W. Adams and Eleanor J. Deveau

Volume 1
Factors Influencing Children and Adolescents'
Perceptions and Attitudes Toward Death

Volume 2
Helping Children and Adolescents
Cope with Life-Threatening Illness and Dying

Volume 3
Helping Children and Adolescents Cope with
Death and Bereavement